NAPOLEONIC
LIVES

FAMILY HISTORY FROM PEN & SWORD

Tracing Your Yorkshire Ancestors
Rachel Bellerby

The Great War Handbook
Geoff Bridger

Tracing Your Royal Marine Ancestors
Richard Brooks and Matthew Little

Tracing Your Pauper Ancestors
Robert Burlison

Tracing Your East End Ancestors
Jane Cox

Tracing Your Labour Movement Ancestors
Mark Crail

Tracing Your Ancestors
Simon Fowler

Tracing Your Army Ancestors
Simon Fowler

A Guide to Military History on the Internet
Simon Fowler

Tracing Your Northern Ancestors
Keith Gregson

Your Irish Ancestors
Ian Maxwell

Tracing Your Northern Irish Ancestors
Ian Maxwell

Tracing Your Northern Irish Ancestors
Ian Maxwell

Tracing Your Scottish Ancestors
Ian Maxwell

Tracing Your London Ancestors
Jonathan Oates

Tracing Family History on the Internet
Christopher Patton

Great War Lives
Paul Reed

Tracing Your Air Force Ancestors
Phil Tomaselli

Tracing Your Secret Service Ancestors
Phil Tomaselli

Tracing Your Criminal Ancestors
Stephen Wade

Tracing Your Legal Ancestors
Stephen Wade

Tracing Your Police Ancestors
Stephen Wade

Tracing Your Jewish Ancestors
Rosemary Wenzerul

Fishing and Fishermen
Martin Wilcox

How Our Ancestors Lived

NAPOLEONIC LIVES

*Researching the British Soldiers
of the Napoleonic Wars*

Carole Divall

Pen & Sword
FAMILY HISTORY

First published in Great Britain in 2012 by
PEN & SWORD FAMILY HISTORY
An imprint of
Pen & Sword Books Ltd
47 Church Street
Barnsley
South Yorkshire
S70 2AS

ISBN 978-1-84884-574-9

Typeset by Concept, Huddersfield, West Yorkshire.
Printed and bound in England by CPI Group (UK) Ltd, Croydon, CR0 4YY.

Pen & Sword Books Ltd incorporates the imprints of
Pen & Sword Aviation, Pen & Sword Family History, Pen & Sword Maritime,
Pen & Sword Military, Pen & Sword Discovery, Wharncliffe Local History,
Wharncliffe True Crime, Wharncliffe Transport, Pen & Sword Select,
Pen & Sword Military Classics, Leo Cooper, The Praetorian Press,
Remember When, Seaforth Publishing and Frontline Publishing.

For a complete list of Pen & Sword titles please contact
PEN & SWORD BOOKS LIMITED
47 Church Street, Barnsley, South Yorkshire, S70 2AS, England
E-mail: enquiries@pen-and-sword.co.uk
Website: www.pen-and-sword.co.uk

CONTENTS

ACKNOWLEDGEMENTS

Exploring the lives of a group of men and women, disparate in every respect except for their shared involvement in the Revolutionary and Napoleonic Wars, has been a fascinating and challenging experience. My first thanks, therefore, belong to Rupert Harding. Not only did he suggest that I should write this book, he has also offered unfailing encouragement throughout its composition. Similarly, I also owe thanks to Simon Fowler whose expertise in the field of family research has proved invaluable.

Inevitably, anyone who engages in historical research, of whatever kind, will find themselves needing to consult the collections of documents and other material held by archives and museums. I have been fortunate in the help I have received over a period of time from the staff of The National Archives and the National Army Museum, while a single visit to Lowestoft Museum provided me with a wealth of material. Even where an institution has been consulted by telephone or email, the response has always been generous of time and effort. Thanks are particularly due to the staff of St George's Chapel Archives, Windsor for information on the Military Knights and to the Somerset Family History Society, who provided information on William Wheeler.

I have also received help from individuals who have been prepared to give up their time on my behalf. Julian Fane's knowledge of his family, willingly shared, made writing about the Fanes of Fulbeck particularly rewarding. John Macdonald freely shared the information in his possession relevant to Thomas Walker Chambers. Stella Child, on behalf of the Bexhill Hanoverian Study Group, patiently answered every query I sent her. Lieutenant-Colonel John Downham has been unfailing in his support since I first started my researches into the 30th Foot and he was able yet again to give me those captivating snippets which bring history to life, particularly as both the 30th and 59th regiments were constituent units of the Queen's Lancashire Regiment, now amalgamated into the Duke of Lancaster's Regiment. Janet and David Bromley have spent years compiling their register of memorials of the period. Consequently, they were able to explain to me why Andrew Hartley became a knight of Windsor.

Sometimes people provide valuable information without realising it. Patrick Mercer and Ian Fletcher may well have wondered why I listened so intently to their lectures on the artillery and cavalry respectively. They will find the answer in this book.

Help can also arrive unexpectedly. An Australian internet contact, Shirley Sweetland Skinner, was kind enough to search for Samuel Lickler in the Australian records when my own searches had proved fruitless.

Accessing appropriate illustrations is crucial to a book of this kind, and my thanks go to Emily Lefley of the Image Library at the National Army Museum for her efforts on my behalf. I also owe a debt of gratitude to Philip Haythornthwaite who, once again, has generously made available his own collections of pictures, and to Mick Crumplin, who has done likewise. Some images have proved particularly difficult to find in the public domain, so I cannot omit making reference to the generosity of Messrs Storey's Ltd (www.storeysltd.co.uk), who freely made some of their prints available.

Finally, I am, as always, indebted to my husband who has produced the maps for this book and has photographed much of the original material that is reproduced here, as well as undertaking some of the trawling through the records on our joint visits to The National Archives.

INTRODUCTION
The Revolutionary and Napoleonic Wars
1792–1815

On 28 April 1792 a French army, nearly 20,000 strong and under the command of Marshal Rochambeau, crossed the border into the Austrian Netherlands (modern Belgium). Its objective was simple: to export revolution. Although France was officially still a monarchy, the extremists were merely biding their time and the country would soon sink into the chaos of the Reign of Terror. This first campaign of 1792 was brief and ended in ignominious failure but it strengthened the determination of the sovereigns of Europe to deal the revolutionaries a fatal blow before their thrones also began to totter. Austria and Prussia launched a joint invasion of France in August 1792, thus setting in motion a war which lasted until 1815, with only one brief interval of peace.

This first 'Great War' convulsed the whole of Europe, from Britain to the Bosphorus and spread to wherever the major European powers had foreign interests, even drawing in the fledgling United States of America. Its greatest hero, Napoleon Bonaparte, gave his name to both a war and an era. In Britain, victories were won by arguably our greatest admiral and greatest general, Nelson and Wellington.

Britain was initially reluctant to become involved. The Prime Minister, William Pitt, was more concerned with putting right the financial catastrophe of the war with the American colonists, which had come to an end only nine years before. After the execution of Louis XVI in January 1793, however, war with France was inevitable. Even then it was the Convention of Paris that declared war on Britain, Spain and the Netherlands, and launched an attack on the Dutch.

The result was a British campaign in the Netherlands which ended miserably and is best remembered for the children's rhyme commemorating *The Grand Old Duke of York*. Nor was an Anglo-Spanish attempt to aid the Royalists of Toulon any more successful, although there was a change of fortune in Corsica, as Samuel Rockliffe of the 69th discovered while serving as a marine. Furthermore, although

1

the other continental powers initially achieved success against the ill-organised French Army, by 1794 the revolution had been saved by a *Levée en Masse* (conscription of all males). Britain continued to gain victories at sea, but campaigns on land ended in failure, including another Dutch expedition. Yet as Daniel Nicol of the 92nd (Gordon Highlanders) and Benjamin Miller of the Royal Artillery vividly recorded in their diaries, there was some success in Egypt in 1801 when the French were forced to surrender both Cairo and Alexandria.

In France, Napoleon Bonaparte, who first attracted attention at the siege of Toulon and then conducted a successful campaign against the Austrians in northern Italy, manoeuvred himself into the position of First Consul in 1799. Three years later he was elected Consul for life, and two years after that, emperor. By 1808 Europe was at his feet. After Austerlitz (1805), perhaps the high point of his military career, the Holy Roman Empire was consigned to history. Prussia was crushed at Jena-Auerstädt in 1806. Russia was brought to heel by the Treaty of Tilsit a year later. Only Britain remained at war. The Continental System was designed to starve Britain of its trading lifeblood by closing all mainland European ports to British ships. When the system was extended from allies of France to neutral nations, it seemed that Napoleon's triumph was complete. There was no reason to believe that Denmark, Sweden and Portugal would resist his diktat.

A successful expedition (of doubtful legitimacy) in 1807 deprived the Danes of their navy before the French could seize it. An attempt to assist the Swedes in their resistance proved impossible in a country where the king was madly unstable. Portugal, however, was a different matter. The ports of Lisbon and Oporto remained conduits for British goods into the whole of Iberia and beyond. Thus Portugal became the object of Napoleon's wrath. He also took the opportunity, however, to replace the degenerate Spanish royal family with his eldest brother, Joseph. Thus, as he later acknowledged, he created the 'Spanish ulcer' which along with the misguided invasion of Russia in 1812 sowed the seeds for his eventual defeat.

The Peninsular War (1808–14), known to the Spanish as the War of Independence, gave the British Army the chance to demonstrate what could be achieved under talented commanders, Sir John Moore and Sir Arthur Wellesley (later Duke of Wellington). Nicol saw action there, as did Thomas Walker Chambers of the 30th. The former became a prisoner of the French. The latter nearly died at the bloody siege of Badajoz. Benjamin Harris, Tom Plunkett and Edward Costello, serving with the elite light division, considered themselves first into action and last out. William Wheeler was with the 7th division, unkindly labelled the mongrels because of the presence of so many foreign units. His letters to his mother convey both the good times and the bad times of a soldier's life. Thomas Jarvis encountered the particular difficulties of the cavalry, at their worse during the retreat to Corunna, a nightmare experience shared by Benjamin Miller. Andrew Hartley of the Horse Guards recorded his experiences in conditions similarly inimical to the mounted soldier in the last months of the Peninsular War. Away to the south Robert Cairnes of the Royal Horse Artillery was involved in the siege of Cadiz.

A war which dragged on for over twenty years engaged whole families, like the Fanes of Fulbeck. Nor should women be forgotten. Mrs Reston demonstrated extreme courage under fire, while Mrs Skiddy was one of many women who were prepared to risk the anger of Wellington himself in her determination to make life comfortable for her husband.

Although Napoleon fought a fierce campaign in 1813, by the end of the year the combined might of the old monarchies meant that his days as emperor were numbered. In April 1814 he abdicated and sailed into exile on the island of Elba, while the victorious powers assembled in Vienna to re-draw the map of Europe. Ever the gambler, however, Napoleon risked one further throw of the dice. He returned to France in March 1815 and assembled yet another army. To survive he needed to defeat the two nearest allied armies, Anglo-Dutch under the Duke of Wellington and Prussian under Marshal Blücher, before the Austrians and Russians could threaten his eastern frontier.

A strategically brilliant advance, which wrong-footed his opponents, ended in tactical disaster at Waterloo on 18 June 1815. Inevitably, some 'Napoleonic Lives' ended on this battlefield. Although there was some further mopping-up, the Revolutionary and Napoleonic wars were effectively over, ending where they had started, in Belgium. Napoleon was sent to St Helena, in the middle of the Atlantic, where he died in 1821.

A war of such magnitude inevitably caused heavy casualties, even though battles were small by modern standards. Although the figures remain estimates, it is generally agreed that there were between 2,500,000 and 3,500,000 military deaths, most of them off the battlefield, while total casualties including civilians could be as high as 6,000,000.

The effects on Britain and its army were also dramatic. In 1793 the British Army numbered about 40,000 men in the three arms of artillery, cavalry and infantry. By 1813 the number had risen to 250,000 men, in a population of no more than 9,000,000. There was also a large Militia, designed for home service. Most people researching their family history will find a soldier of the period in their ancestry.

Wellington famously remarked that his army was 'the scum of the earth', although he added, 'It is really wonderful that we should have made them the fine fellows they are.' Every commanding officer knew, however, that his unit contained a number of the 'king's hard bargains'. Richard Key and Samuel Lickler deserve this label but they also represent the experience of another kind of soldier, the man who found himself sent to an alien outpost with only alcohol to distract him from the tedium of military life without action.

The popular perception at the time of Britain's volunteer army was not complimentary. It was assumed with some justice that only the desperate and the destitute would enlist for a shilling a day, most of which was deducted in stoppages. It was obvious to all but the enlightened few that such men needed the lash to keep them in order and drill to turn them into military automatons. Yet these men covered themselves in glory on battlefields from Egypt to Portugal, which suggests that the stereotypical view, like all stereotypes, tells only a part of the truth. The following case studies sometimes reinforce but more often challenge the stereotype while at the same time they recreate, however selectively, something of what it was like to serve king and country during the first Great War.

A GUIDE TO RESEARCHING THE REVOLUTIONARY AND NAPOLEONIC WARS

The summary which follows each case study and suggests how the information may be accessed should provide some pertinent guidelines on how to research the men (and their families) who served in the British Army at the end of the eighteenth and the beginning of the nineteenth century. Nevertheless, a more general overview will provide a wider range of possible routes for the family historian to follow.

The War Office was the recipient of regimental and other records. These are now lodged at The National Archives in Kew (www.nationalarchives.gov.uk). Access is freely available upon production of photo identity such as a driving licence or passport, and a domestic bill to prove residence. (If you are not a British citizen, a passport is required.) This gives you a reader's ticket so that you can access any document in the collection. In a recent re-organisation, however, the records most frequently consulted by family historians, which have been digitised, can be consulted without a reader's ticket. An initial visit spent in the open section should not only prove a useful orientating experience but will also enable you to seek the help and advice of the expert staff.

If you know in which regiment, or regiments, your ancestor served, the obvious starting point is his discharge papers, assuming he survived and was granted a pension. If he was discharged at Chelsea, the relevant reference is WO97. These papers have been digitised and can be accessed by name and regiment. Be warned, though, there are some omissions. If he was discharged at Kilmainham, the reference is WO119. Unfortunately, these records have not been digitised, so you have to trawl through chronological but otherwise somewhat random papers to find what you want. The place of discharge, incidentally, has nothing to do with nationality but depends upon where the regiment was serving when your forebear was discharged.

If you find his discharge papers, you will discover where he was born, where and when he enlisted, his age upon enlistment, his occupation before enlistment, length of service, reason for discharge, and a comment on his conduct. There will also be a brief description: height, colour of hair and eyes, and complexion, intended to prevent fraudulent pension claims.

If your ancestor did not survive the war he will be in the regiment's casualty returns, specific to the battalion in which he served. After 1808 these became more detailed and will tell you when and where he died, sometimes giving the exact circumstances. In some cases his place of birth and enlistment and his trade will also be included. Another point of interest may be the amount of money he left and to whom he left it. This may provide the names of his wife and children. Soldiers were increasingly encouraged to make wills and although many of these are simple statements, others contain moving evidence of concern for orphaned children and trust in the promises of friends to protect their interests. The reference for casualty returns is WO25. There is a register which was started in 1799, also WO25, which gives brief details (date and place of death) but notes circumstances if other than natural. The casualty returns also list deserters, thus explaining a possibly mysterious disappearance from a regiment.

If neither discharge papers nor casualty returns provide what you are looking for, or if your forebear died before 1799, your next step is to examine the muster rolls/pay lists, for which the reference is WO12. You will probably want to consult these anyway because they will tell you what he was doing on a month-by-month basis. Possible information includes periods of sickness, imprisonment or time spent on detached command and recruiting duties. They will also tell you if he came into the regiment from the Militia, and when and why he departed. This might include transfer to a different regiment. The muster rolls also detail all promotions to and reductions from drummer/trumpeter, corporal or sergeant.

Should your ancestor prove to be an officer, different tactics need to be adopted. Some muster rolls include information on the officers of the battalion: arrival and departure, for whatever reason, sickness, periods of leave or on detached duties, periods spent 'under an arrest' or 'under sentence of a court martial'. Other muster rolls do not even include which officers were present. The 30th Regiment exemplifies this. The first battalion in India continued to use an older form of muster roll and noted all the information listed above. The second battalion in Ireland, then the Peninsula and Flanders, used the replacement, less detailed form. To find information of this and similar battalions it is necessary to consult the monthly returns (WO17). These reveal the movements of the battalion, and also its strength on a monthly basis, as well as giving precise details of what the officers were doing, including detached duties.

The monthly returns also note promotions, although an easier way to trace an officer's career, often through several regiments, is by means of the annual Army Lists. These are available at both The National Archives and in the reading room of the National Army Museum, Chelsea (www.national-army-museum.ac.uk). They may also be held in central libraries or archives. Even more interesting, however, are officers' statements of service, found in WO25 (which you will have realised by now is a compendious file). The first collection covers 1809–10 and is arranged alphabetically. In 1828 retired officers on full or half-pay gave details of their first commission, subsequent service, marriage and children. The same information was collected a year later for serving officers. WO25 also includes details of officers who served on the staff, both at home and abroad, and of medical officers, including the training received by surgeons. WO31 contains applications to purchase and sell commissions, sometimes supported by personal family information and letters of recommendation.

If your officer forebear was a casualty, including being wounded, a useful book is Volume VIII of *A History of the Peninsular War: The Biographical Dictionary of British Officers Killed and Wounded 1808–1814*, compiled by John A. Hall. Should your forebear have attained the rank of major or higher, *The Royal Military Calendar of Army Service and Commission Book*, published in 1820, will give you details of his career. This is available in a modern reprint.

It is possible your ancestor may prove to be one of the 'king's hard bargains', in which case WO93, an index of general court-martial records, will tell you whether his offences were serious enough for him to have stood a general court martial. The proceedings can be found in WO71, but these papers are stored in boxes arranged only by date and not all the records have survived. If you are lucky, though, you will not only be able to read the full details of the case, you will also 'hear' the man's voice in the verbatim report. On the other hand, he may only have stood regimental courts martial.

Records of these began to appear in inspection returns in 1811. They detail the offence, the sentence and the actual punishment inflicted.

Obviously, with such a wealth of material to choose from as possible starting points, a handbook as a guide is a useful tool. *Army Records for Family Historians*, a National Archives guide by Simon Fowler and William Spencer, exhaustively details what is available, illustrated by some case studies. *Tracing your Ancestors in the National Archives* by Amanda Bevan includes army records along with everything else held at Kew.

The internet is an invaluable tool for family historians, as *A Guide to Military History on the Internet* by Simon Fowler makes clear. The catalogues of The National Archives and many military and local museums and archives can be accessed, giving the researcher a clear idea of what is available where. Then there are the genealogy sites such as Ancestry (www.ancestry.co.uk) and Find My Past (www.findmypast.co.uk). Some areas of these sites require subscription, however. More generally, Wikipedia (www.wikipedia.org) contains a wealth of information on battles, casualties and personalities and in this area is generally unbiased, although not always reliable. Sometimes inaccurate information which has appeared in a book or on another site is merely replicated. Such information should always be cross-checked with other sources. A more specialist site is the international Napoleonic Series (www.napoleon-series.org). Genuki (UK and Ireland Genealogical Service), which is both a resource and a gateway to other resources, has *Military History* and *Military Records* as specific subject headings. The Website www.Familysearch.org or the International Genealogical Index which can be accessed at www.ancestor-search.info/SRC-IGI.htm are useful for more general research.

The first medal awarded to all ranks was the Waterloo medal, presented in 1816 to the survivors, and to the families of those killed if they made the necessary application. The roll of names, arranged by regiment and then usually by company, can be found at The National Archives in WO100. It is available on microfilm. There is also a published version which can be found in some libraries and archives. This is complemented by *The Waterloo Roll Call* (John Dalton), which focuses on officers and includes some biographical detail.

The award of this medal (and the two-year pension enhancement) was bitterly resented by men who had fought for as many as six years in the Peninsula but whose units were not at Waterloo. Despite many appeals to the authorities it was not until 1847 that the first military General Service Medal (with a naval equivalent) was instituted, with bars for actions dating back to the Revolutionary Wars. Unfortunately, many of the combatants were long dead by this time. Also some survivors did not apply, so if your forebear's name is not found in the roll, even if he survived to 1847, he may still have been present at some of the actions. This medal roll can also be found in WO100 and in printed form.

Local newspapers flourished in many areas in the late eighteenth and early nineteenth centuries and may contain information that illuminates your ancestor's experiences. When researching the wreck of the *Queen*, which was bringing soldiers and prisoners of war back from the Peninsula, I discovered detailed accounts in two Cornish newspapers, as well as a briefer account in *The Times*. Similarly, the *Limerick Evening Post* contained detailed accounts of the first Waterloo anniversary celebrations held by the 30th Foot in 1816. National events would, of course, be reported in the London and national papers like *The Times* and the *Morning Chronicle*. The British Library at Colindale, north London (www.bl.uk/aboutus/quickinfo/loc/colindale/index) holds a large collection of national and local newspapers of the period which are now being made available online, while issues of *The Times* are also available online. The *London Gazette* is not only a useful general source but also contains information on promotions and casualties (killed and wounded). Periodicals like the *Gentleman's Magazine* often included obituaries of higher-ranked officers and as time passed, local newspapers noted the deaths of their Napoleonic celebrities.

Unlike the major wars of the twentieth century, there are no war memorials for the Revolutionary and Napoleonic Wars. There are individual memorials, however, mainly to officers, and some still legible gravestones. These have been recorded, with illustrations, by David and Janet Bromley of the Waterloo Association, and recently published by Pen & Sword. Such a resource will prove invaluable to the family history researcher.

Other rich storehouses of material are the military and local museums and archives already referred to. Consult a handbook like the one produced by the Army Museums Ogilby Trust (*The AMOT Guide to Military Museums in the UK 2011–2012*) or trawl the internet (www.armymuseums.org.uk and www.culture24.org.uk are good starting points) and you will quickly discover what is available. A practical problem has been caused by the many amalgamations of regiments since 1815. A search on the internet, however, using the regiment's number in 1815 will reveal its present embodiment. Many of these museums have copies of War Office documents, particularly WO97 and WO100, as well as books and handwritten accounts specific to their constituent units.

Finally, and obviously, whatever your ancestor's geographical origins, there will almost certainly be a member of the appropriate local or family history society who will be able to give you valuable background information, if not specific details.

TIMELINE

B ritish involvement in the Revolutionary and Napoleonic Wars, with some other major events as points of reference. Italics indicate events in which the subjects of this book were involved.

1789   Storming of the Bastille, symbolic start of the French Revolution.

1792   Proclamation of the French Republic.

1793   Execution of Louis XVI. France declares war on Holland and Britain. Unsuccessful British expedition to the Low Countries. Admiral Hood puts British troops into Toulon.

1794   *The British capture Corsica.*

        Fall of the Jacobins in France.

1795   Napoleon appointed commander-in-chief in Italy and defeats the Austrians.

1796   Spain declares war on Britain.

1797   Peace of Campo Formio between France and Austria.

        Battle of Cape St Vincent: British defeat a Spanish fleet.

1798   French expedition to Egypt. Battle of the Pyramids: French defeat an Ottoman army.

        Battle of the Nile: French fleet destroyed by Nelson.

1799   Napoleon fails to take Acre; returns to France. Austria declares war on France.

        British expedition to the Netherlands.

1800   Napoleon appointed First Consul.

1801   Peace of Lunéville between France and Austria.

        Battle of Alexandria: Abercromby defeats the French; surrender of Cairo and Alexandria; French leave Egypt.

1802   Napoleon becomes First Consul for life. Peace of Amiens between Britain and France.

1803   Renewal of war between Britain and France. *French occupy Hanover.*

        Battle of Assaye: Sir Arthur Wellesley defeats the Mahratta Confederation.

1804 Napoleon proclaimed Emperor.

Spain declares war on Britain.

1805 Battle of Austerlitz: Napoleon defeats a combined Austro-Russian army.

Battle of Trafalgar: Nelson defeats a Franco-Spanish fleet.

1806 Battles of Jena and Auerstädt: Napoleon defeats the Prussians.

Napoleon establishes the Continental System to destroy British trade.

1807 Battle of Friedland: Napoleon defeats the Russians; Treaty of Tilsit with the Russians enables him to extend the Continental System.

France invades neutral Portugal to close the last continental ports to Britain.

1808 France invades Spain; Napoleon makes his brother Joseph King of Spain; beginning of the Peninsular War.

Battles of Roliça and Vimeiro: Sir Arthur Wellesley defeats the French.

1809 *Battle of Corunna: Sir John Moore defeats the French; British evacuate Spain.*

War between France and Austria; Peace of Schönbrunn brings Austria into the Continental System.

Battles of Oporto and Talavera: Wellesley defeats the French.

1810 *French besiege Cadiz; Sir Thomas Graham commands British forces.*

Battle of Buçaco: Wellington defeats the French; *retreats to the Lines of Torres Vedras.*

1811 *Battle of Barrosa: Graham defeats the French.*

French retreat from Portugal. Battle of Fuentes de Oñoro: Wellington defeats the French. Battle of Albuera: allied army under Marshal Beresford defeats the French.

1812 *Wellington takes Ciudad Rodrigo and Badajoz. Battle of Salamanca: Wellington defeats the French. Triumphant entry into Madrid. Failed siege of Burgos and retreat to Portugal.*

Napoleon invades Russia; retreats from Moscow when Russians refuse to come to terms.

United States declares war on Britain.

1813   Prussia and Austria declare war on France. Battle of Leipzig: northern allies defeat Napoleon.

Battle of Vitoria: Wellington defeats the French. By the end of the year Anglo-Portuguese and Spanish forces are in southern France.

1814   Napoleon defeated in a series of engagements against the northern allies.

Battle of Toulouse: Wellington defeats the French.

Napoleon abdicates; Louis XVIII proclaimed king. Congress of Vienna to re-draw the map of Europe.

Treaty of Ghent ends the war between Britain and the United States.

1815   Napoleon escapes from Elba and returns to France in triumph.

Battle of Quatre Bras: Wellington defeats Marshal Ney. Battle of Ligny: Napoleon defeats Marshal Blücher and the Prussians.

Battle of Waterloo: Wellington and Blücher defeat Napoleon.

Napoleon's second abdication and exile on St Helena.

Chapter One

SOLDIER AT SEA
Samuel Rockliffe of the 69th

When Samuel Rockliffe enlisted in the 69th (South Lincoln-shire) Regiment it was inevitable that he would soon find himself fighting the French. Pitt and the British government may have thought it would be possible to remain detached from events in France, but that was to misunderstand the nature of revolution. By December 1792, when Rockliffe attested, those who were directing the revolution were committed to exporting their ideas to peoples still oppressed by reactionary regimes. There had already been an abortive attempt to invade the Austrian Netherlands (modern Belgium). On 1 February 1793, after the execution of Louis XVI, the revolutionaries declared war against Holland and Britain. For Rockliffe, however, active service would take him not to war on land but to service at sea.

The Navy was both the bulwark of Britain's defences and the preferred instrument of her aggressive power, but ships required men, both sailors and marines. These latter were needed to enforce discipline below decks and prevent mutiny. In 1793 there were too few marines to go round, so regular soldiers were drafted in. Consequently, men of the 69th were sent in detachments to *Britannia*, *Courageux*, *Berwick*, *Agamemnon*, *Ardent* and *Audacious*, all part of the Mediterranean fleet under Sir Samuel Hood on his flagship, *Victory*.

Under normal circumstances, Rockliffe's duties as a marine en-compassed guard duty, particularly guarding the powder room, standing guard when punishment was inflicted, summoning the men to dinner with the beat of a drum (although the marines messed separately), and helping to heave the capstans or serve the officers when not on duty. Should the fleet go into action, he could be required to help man the guns, clamber into the rigging as a sharp-shooter, or form part of a boarding party.

Rockliffe went aboard the 64-gun *Agamemnon* (popularly known as *Eggs-and-Bacon*) in April 1793 along with two sergeants and fifty-three other ranks, under the command of Captain John Clarke and Lieutenant John McClintock, joining the fifteen marines already aboard. Commanded by her new captain, Horatio Nelson, *Agamemnon* left Chatham on 24 April, probably before Rockliffe and his fellows had time to adapt to their new conditions. They sailed past the Nore, on to Spithead, and then to the Scilly Isles where they joined the main fleet. Their voyage took them south to Cape St Vincent and on through the Straits of Gibraltar. Britain was in alliance with Spain at this time, and *Agamemnon* was one of six ships allowed to water at Cadiz. The captains were invited ashore. It is unlikely that the invitation was extended to the seamen and marines, although it was usual practice for marines to be drilled on shore whenever a ship was in port. Even if it was from on board, Rockliffe undoubtedly took a good look at Europe's largest and wealthiest port.

What had so far been an uneventful voyage became something quite different in August when the fleet was close to Toulon, base of the French Mediterranean fleet. Hood's mission was to blockade the port. When two envoys arrived from Marseille, which had risen against Jacobin rule, begging for British assistance, he initially refused, but a day later he was persuaded to act by a second delegation. The rashness of this decision, which was influenced by a promise that Toulon would rise against the Jacobins, was demonstrated two days later when the uprising in Marseille was ruthlessly crushed. Hood might have twenty-three ships of the line and fourteen frigates but the only troops available were the soldiers serving as marines, not all of whom could be released from the ships. And troops were needed to defend Toulon against the triumphant Jacobins.

Although 1,200 soldiers and 200 sailors were landed without opposition, Hood also looked about for reinforcements, sending messages to Gibraltar, to his Spanish allies (who quickly supplied twelve ships and 3,000 men), to Sardinia, Austria and Naples. This last message was carried by *Agamemnon*, keeping Rockliffe on board rather than being part of the increasingly pressurised defence of Toulon. By 5 October, *Agamemnon* was back at Toulon with promise of reinforcements, but only three days later she again set sail, to join Commodore Robert Linzee's squadron off Sardinia. Rockliffe was about to hear naval guns fired in anger.

At 2.00am on 22 October a convoy of five ships was sighted, and preparations were made for action. By 4.00am the French ships were within gunshot range. There followed a three-hour engagement with the *Melpomène* during which, because of sickness among the crew of *Agamemnon*, the men of the 69th helped man the guns. A wind shift eventually enabled *Melpomène* to sail out of range, but so disabled that a French frigate had to take her in tow. She had twenty-four men dead, against one on board *Agamemnon*. No doubt Rockliffe shared the view of a 12-year-old midshipman, William Hoste, that Captain Nelson was acknowledged as one of the first characters in the Service, and was universally beloved by his men and officers.

Nelson had brought orders from Hood for Linzee to sail to Tunis and persuade the Bey, who operated in the piratical fashion of his forebears, to spare British shipping as he spared French (it was suspected that the French paid protection money). The expedition was a failure, but the five days spent in the port of Tunis gave Rockliffe yet more matter to report back to his family when he next saw them. Yet, with only brief periods at anchor since leaving the Nore, the tedium of shipboard life was affecting everyone from Nelson downward. The soldiers, knowing nothing of what was happening in Toulon, must have been envious of their land-based comrades. However, while *Agamemnon* was at Livorno (Leghorn) charged with protecting British shipping from French predators, news arrived of the evacuation and fall of Toulon, with losses to the 69th.

Forced out of Toulon, Hood now used Corsica as his base, and quickly became involved in Corsican politics on the side of those who wished to free the island from French rule. When a planned raid by Corsican patriots failed, Hood set up a blockade and attacked shore batteries. At the end of December *Agamemnon* was brought from Livorno to take part in these activities but sailed into a storm, 'the hardest gale of wind almost ever remembered here. The *Agamemnon* did well but lost every sail in her.'[1] Nevertheless, on 21 January 1794 Nelson landed sixty soldiers and sailors near San Fiorenzo and Rockliffe had his first taste of direct action against the French, although it amounted to no more than burning a mill and destroying a stock of flour. Despite being pursued by French gunboats, the whole party returned safely.

This was the pattern for the next two weeks, but on 7 February a more decisive action took place when troops under General Dundas

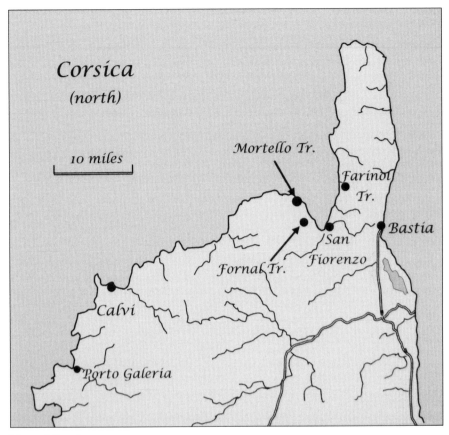

Map of Corsica.

attacked the Tower of Mortello, which surrendered after a day, and then San Fiorenzo, which also fell. Joint army and navy operations had a tendency to descend into wrangling and it quickly became apparent that Corsica would be no exception. Hood now identified taking Bastia as the next objective but Dundas was determined to wait for reinforcements, 2,000 men expected from Gibraltar, before committing himself further, so Hood had to content himself with a demonstration against Bastia. This did not stop Nelson making three runs inshore and destroying six French guns. He also landed an artillery officer and an engineer under cover of darkness to recon-noitre the best landing place and sites for shore batteries.

On 3 April 1,284 officers and men, naval and military, under the command of Nelson and Lieutenant-Colonel Villettes of the 69th, were landed north of Bastia. While Hood moored the fleet around the harbour but out of reach of the French shore batteries, the 'Agamemnons' (sailors and soldiers) brought eight of the ship's 24-pounder guns and eight 13-inch mortars ashore. They established camp only 2,500 yards from the citadel, cleared the ground, built roads and hauled guns into position using pulleys and tackle, seaman-fashion, an operation which was now familiar to Rockliffe and his fellow soldiers. The landing of supplies continued without interruption, and on 11 April the guns opened fire. The bombardment was kept up all night. The French retaliated, and Nelson was among those hit, although the wound did not put him out of action. In total, five men from *Agamemnon* were lost.

Eventually on 21 May, after a siege which had lasted thirty-seven days with four further days of negotiation, Bastia surrendered. Two days later the army took possession of the town gates, implicitly claiming the victory. Despite being a soldier, Rockliffe must have shared the resentment of the other Agamemnons, but he could rejoice in the part he had played in acquiring Corsica for King George. On the other hand, it might have pleased him that Lieutenant-Colonel Villettes of his regiment became the governor of Bastia.

Full possession of Corsica, however, required possession of Calvi. Although *Agamemnon* sailed to Gibraltar for a desperately needed refit, by mid-June she was anchored off Porto Galeria, just south of Calvi. Nelson was now in command of naval forces, while the army was under the command of Lieutenant-Colonel the Honourable Charles Stuart in a joint operation. Reconnaissance revealed that Calvi was strongly positioned and strongly defended. Despite this, men, guns and supplies were safely landed and the first battery was operational by 4 July. Two other batteries quickly followed. Indeed, the main problem was sickness, not efficiency, as a malarial-type fever quickly spread among the men. For the French, though, the speed with which the enemy had brought up their guns across impossible terrain left them unprepared for the attack which followed.

The French focused on destroying the British guns, and managed to disable three. During one of these attacks a splinter of stone cost Nelson the sight of one eye, although he refused to leave the front line. On 19 July one of the French defensive positions, Fort Muzello, was taken and its guns turned on the town. The governor, recognising his hopeless position, negotiated a twenty-five-day peace.

He was hoping for reinforcements but when none had arrived by 10 August he surrendered. Two days later Nelson and his sailors and soldiers returned to *Agamemnon*.

Corsica was Rockliffe's only experience of land-based action. At sea there were blockading duties and refits, interrupted by moments of excitement. Foul weather was always a trial, but as Nelson wrote to his wife: 'In *Agamemnon* we mind nothing. She is the finest ship I ever sailed in ...'[2] On 10 March 1795 an action seemed likely between seventeen French ships of the line and fourteen British but the French sailed over the horizon before the British could form line of battle. The next day, however, *Agamemnon* came upon the already damaged *Ça Ira*. The dramatic 'beat to quarters' soon had the decks cleared for action. Some of the marines were with the guns; others stood pistol in hand guarding the hatchways so that the powder monkeys and messengers could scurry backwards and forwards. Manoeuvring skilfully as the *Ça Ira* struggled to fire a broadside, *Agamemnon* was able to pound the wounded ship into a complete wreck. Dependent upon a tow from the frigate, *Vestale*, she would have become a British prize if Admiral Hotham, in command, had not signalled the recall. *Agamemnon* had seven wounded casualties against 100 dead and wounded on *Ça Ira*, which was taken the following day, along with *Censeur*, by two other British ships. Because prizes meant money, Rockliffe knew what he lost through Hotham's caution, which had allowed the other French ships to get off safely.

Yet another such opportunity was scuppered by Hotham when *Agamemnon* and three other ships came upon the rear of the French Mediterranean fleet. *Victory* and *Culloden* went into action but as *Agamemnon* and *Cumberland* sailed into firing range Hotham again raised the signal to retire. In August, however, *Agamemnon*, along with six frigates, raided Alessio and seized ten French vessels. Fortunately, Hotham was off the scene.

By June 1796 *Agamemnon* was ordered to England for a complete refit. At the same time, the poor health of Captain Smith of HMS *Captain* sent him back to England. Thus on 13 June Commodore Nelson, as he now was, raised his pennant on the 74-gun *Captain*. With him went the men of the 69th, who joined fourteen men of the 11th on a ship with no regular marines.

The first task of the new command was a miserable one, supervision of the evacuation of Corsica. Erstwhile ally, Spain, was now

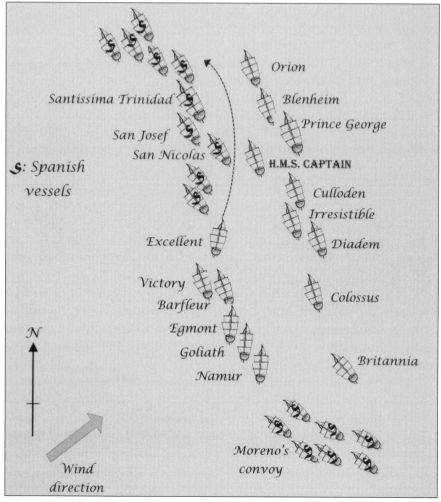

Battle of Cape St Vincent.

Britain's enemy, as was much of Italy. Consequently, it was impossible for a British fleet to maintain a presence in the Mediterranean. And Rockliffe would next find himself in action not against the French but against the Spanish.

On 13 February 1797 Nelson brought HMS *Captain* to join Admiral Jervis's fleet off Cape St Vincent, the western corner of Portugal. He carried news that the Spanish grand fleet, comprising twenty-seven ships of the line and three frigates, was at sea. Among these Spanish ships was the *Santissima Trinidad*, a four-decker, reputedly the largest ship of its time. Although Jervis had only fifteen ships of the line and seven frigates, at sunset he raised the signal to form battle order.

When St Valentine's Day dawned hazily, the British fleet was in complete order, standing on a wind to the SSW. At 6.30am *Culloden* signalled that five Spanish sail had been sighted. Soon after 8.00am the order was given to prepare for battle. By 10.00am twenty sail had been sighted in the SW corner, and a further eight S by W. Within thirty minutes the whole Spanish fleet was visible. It was also obvious that they were manoeuvring to regroup, giving Jervis the opportunity to cut out the temporarily separated ships. The British fleet formed line of battle, a-head and a-stern and steered SSW. At 11.26am the signal was given to engage and four minutes later the firing began, producing the confusion of sound and smoke with which Rockliffe was now familiar, although at a level of ferocity he had never previously experienced.

As the action developed, Jervis signalled: 'Take suitable stations for mutual support and engage the enemy as coming up in succession.' Nelson decided upon a generous interpretation of this order and directed Captain Miller to wear ship, thus taking *Captain* out of the line. She passed between *Diadem* and *Excellent*, and sailed across the bows of six Spanish ships, including the towering *Santissima Trinidad*. Having made herself a target of the enemy's guns, she lost her fore-topmast among other damage. Some respite was offered when *Culloden* and *Excellent* (Captain Collingwood) separately joined in the attack. This allowed *Captain* to replenish her ammunition and undertake some running repairs. Then her wheel was shot away and she became totally unmanageable. Another commander might have struck his flag at this point but Nelson was never a man to back out of a fight.

The nearest Spanish ship was the *San Nicolás*, which was hooked, starboard quarter, to *Captain*'s larboard cat-head, and Nelson decided to board her:

> The word to board being given, the officers and seamen destined for the duty, headed by Lieutenant Berry, together with the detachment of the 69th Regiment, commanded by Lieutenant Pearson ... passed with rapidity on board the enemy's ships; and in a short time the *San Nicolás* was in the possession of her intrepid assailants.[3]

At this point the *San Josef*, which had run into the *San Nicolás*, opened fire on the boarders, whereupon Nelson gave the order to board the second ship. He later wrote in his dispatch:

> The soldiers of the 69th, with an alacrity which will ever do them credit, and Lieutenant Pearson of the same regiment, were almost the foremost in this service ... A soldier of the 69th Regiment having broken the upper quarter-gallery window, I jumped in myself, and was followed by the others as fast as possible.

Some Spanish resistance was quickly dealt with by men who were undoubtedly high on adrenaline, and then 'I passed with my people, and Lieutenant Pearson, on the larboard gangway, to the forecastle, where I met two or three Spanish officers, prisoners of my seamen: they delivered me their swords.' Thus two Spanish ships were taken by the intrepid actions of Nelson, his sailors and soldiers, but *Captain* was the most damaged ship in the British fleet and had taken the heaviest casualties, twenty-four killed (including two soldier-marines from the 11th) and fifty-six wounded.

Cape St Vincent was a glorious and much-needed victory. Four Spanish ships were taken, one of which, the *San Josef*, became Rockliffe's home for the rest of his time at sea as she was sailed back to England. By the end of the year he was once more on dry land. Admirals like Jervis (now Lord Hood) might be rewarded with peerages, but even a humble private could receive acknowledgement of good service. Once the detachment was back with the regiment, Rockliffe was promoted to corporal and then, in December 1799, to sergeant.

It would be pleasing to end Rockliffe's story on this high note, but unfortunately like many NCOs his career pursued a downward trajectory. Six months later, while the 69th were in Ireland, he was demoted, although there is no record of his actual offence. The regiment then went to Jamaica and Rockliffe was given another chance, being made corporal in March 1801 and sergeant seven months later. In March 1802, however, there was another fall from grace and things now went from bad to worse. The following year, after the regiment returned to England, he deserted while on the march from Ipswich to Hull, staying away six weeks. Again, one can only guess his motive, but the march would have taken him the nearest he had been to his family for ten years and temptation may have proved too strong.

Nelson receives the surrender of the *San Josef*. *(Courtesy Messrs Storey's Ltd)*

In 1805 the first battalion of the 69th (the regiment having acquired a second battalion in 1803) sailed to India. Two years later, Rockliffe was dead, almost certainly killed by a combination of climate and disease. For Samuel Rockliffe, his glory days had been spent under the command of England's hero, Horatio Nelson, on British ships of war. Nothing that followed could match such moments as the fall of Bastia, the one-to-one battle with *Ça Ira*, or that glorious St Valentine's Day in 1797 when England's Darling first won the acclaim that became the pattern of his life.

Researching Samuel Rockliffe

The career of Samuel Rockliffe is a good example of both the rewards and the problems of military research. For example, it is relatively easy to establish when he joined the 69th because the date of his attestation as a recruit can be found in the appropriate muster roll for December 1792 (WO12/17695). Where he was recruited remains a mystery, however, because the corresponding monthly return which would contain details of where the recruiting parties were operating has not survived. Indeed, there are no surviving monthly returns for this regiment between 1785 and 1793, a not uncommon situation in the late eighteenth century which makes researching soldiers before the Peace of Amiens (1802) particularly challenging.

Since Rockliffe died in service and does not, therefore, appear in WO97 (Chelsea pension records), we have no biographical details. Nevertheless, by looking at the geographical prevalence of Rockliffe as a surname, using the 1841 census, for example, it is possible to suggest that he came from the eastern part of Lincolnshire. This fits in with his desertion from the ranks while on the march from Ipswich to Hull, and his belated arrival six weeks later. Also, although the county appellations given to regiments in the eighteenth century were often random, the 69th (South Lincolnshire) does seem to have had a closer association with its named geographical area than many other regiments. For example, volunteers were regularly taken in from the Lincolnshire Militia. Although it is unlikely that the parish registers for Lincolnshire would reveal, beyond all doubt, a suitable 'Samuel Rockliffe', they might well suggest several likely candidates. This is also the kind of uncertainty that can often be resolved by consulting the International Genealogical Index although, unfortunately, not in the case of Rockliffe.

Once Rockliffe had enlisted, following his career became straightforward. Although the musters return the men serving on board ship merely as 'on command' or 'with the Mediterranean fleet', the monthly returns (WO17) specify the ships on which they were serving. The next step was to consult the relevant Admiralty documents, ADM35, the pay lists for naval ships, to establish on which ship Rockliffe was serving. Since the detachments from the 69th were distributed among only seven ships, this proved relatively simple. Rockliffe changed ships, of course, from *Agamemnon* to *Captain*, but this was made clear in the records of the former ship.

For anyone who discovers that an ancestor served as a marine and wants to learn more about their experiences, two further primary sources are captains' logs and masters' logs, both to be found in ADM52.

When Rockliffe returned to his regiment in 1798, his career could be followed in detail in the muster rolls. This included his various promotions and demotions, the period of desertion, and his death in

India. Complementing this information, the monthly returns identify where the regiment was serving. Thus it could be established that while the detachments were with the fleet, the rest of the regiment, apart from the recruiting parties, had sailed to the West Indies, where the 'marines' later joined them for a short period before the 69th returned to Europe. Interestingly, the musters make clear that a large number of men chose to stay in the West Indies, transferring into the 55th, 4/60th or one of the West India regiments.

The period of particular interest is the time Rockliffe spent at sea, and here the association with Nelson proved a fortunate factor in adding detail to the bare bones of the ships' pay lists. *Agamemnon* has her own biography (*Nelson's Favourite* by Anthony Deane) while the part played by HMS *Captain* at Cape St Vincent is described in detail in every account of that battle, including the role of the men from the 69th. As a result, it was easy to recreate Rockliffe's experiences while he was a soldier at sea.

Notes
1. Deane, *Nelson's Favourite*, p. 99 (Nelson to his wife).
2. Ibid., p. 113 (Nelson to his wife).
3. King and Hattendorf, *Every Man Will Do His Duty*, p. 77.

Chapter Two

FROM THE SANDS OF EGYPT TO PRISONER OF THE FRENCH

Daniel Nicol of the 92nd

When Daniel Nicol arrived in Edinburgh in March 1794 he was 15 years old and running away from an encounter with the sheriff of Lanark on a poaching charge. For the grandson of a tenant farmer, from Crossford in Lanarkshire, flight was preferable to bringing disgrace on his family. He needed a refuge, however, and he found it in the newly-raised 92nd Foot. Young Daniel enlisted on 12 March, the start of a military career which was to last for twenty years.

The 92nd initially served in Ireland where they found themselves involved in the suppression of the rebellion of 1798. They then formed part of the force which the Duke of York took to Flanders in 1799 for his second ill-fated campaign in the Low Countries. Nicol saw action at Egmont-op-Zoom; he also recognised the mismanagement of the campaign, which finally came to an end in October. The Dutch fleet had been taken, but nothing was achieved on land.

Nicol's next experience of active service was very different. In 1798 the French had sent an expedition to Egypt, part of the Ottoman Empire, hoping it would prove a gateway to India. In command was Napoleon Bonaparte. Although Nelson's victory at the Battle of the Nile (1 August) stranded the French Army, Napoleon achieved notable victories over the Turks, only faltering at the siege of Acre when he took the war into Syria. Politics, however, brought him back to France. General Kléber was left in command and when he was assassinated by a religious fanatic his place was taken by General Menou.

The threat to British India posed by the French occupation of Egypt could not be ignored. At the beginning of 1801 General Sir Ralph Abercromby was sent from Britain while Sir David Baird brought up

Gordon Highlanders. (*Philip Haythornthwaite*)

another force from India in a combined operation to drive out the French. A period was spent in Marmorice Bay practising landings, considered by Nicol an excellent plan which had been wanting in Holland. Abercromby's force then sailed to Aboukir Bay, the scene of Nelson's great victory, and the troops were successfully landed on 8 March, despite French resistance.

The British now advanced towards Alexandria. On 13 March they encountered the French, drawn up in battle order, and the 92nd,

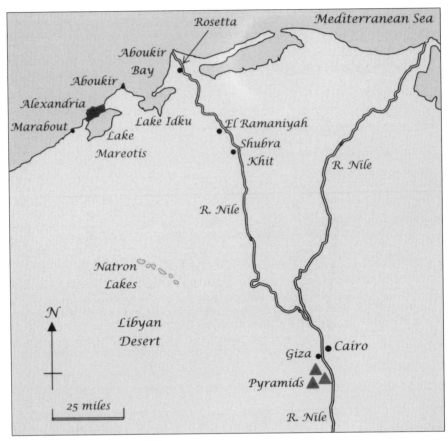

The campaign in Egypt, 1801.

forming the advance guard with the 90th, came under strong attack, losing nearly half their strength, dead and wounded. The French were driven back, however, and preparations were being made for a siege when on the 21st the French again attacked, this time before daybreak. The fierce engagement which followed (the Battle of Alexandria) was the first British victory after eight years of dismal European failure. But Abercromby, 'our worthy commander-in-chief ... was mortally wounded; he died on the 28th, and was deeply regretted by the whole army'.[1]

Abercromby's successor, General Hutchinson, strengthened the position around Alexandria and then, leaving half his force to blockade the city, marched with the other half to face the rest of the French Army, under General Belliard, in Cairo. The French sur-

Death of General Sir Ralph Abercromby. (*Author's collection*)

rendered without a fight on 22 June. 'I believe they were very glad to return to their country,' wrote Nicol. Soon afterwards Baird, who had marched via Suez, reached Cairo. The combined force then returned to Alexandria, which was still holding out.

On 16 August Hutchinson sent a detachment under Sir Eyre Coote to the west of Alexandria. The next day the rest of the army marched onto the plain in front of the city in three divisions. Menou now recognised the gravity of his situation and asked for a three-day cessation of hostilities while he drew up articles of capitulation. On the 29th he asked for another thirty-six hours but Hutchinson gave him until midnight, whereupon he surrendered.

On 11 September the French garrison marched to Aboukir for embarkation to Europe in British ships. Most of the British troops followed soon afterwards to find negotiations under way for a peace settlement, which became the Peace of Amiens (March 1802–May 1803).

So much for the campaign itself but what was it like for the man in the ranks? In his memoirs Nicol made little comment on the conduct of the campaign. Like most soldiers, he was more concerned with his immediate situation, one element of which was the character of his commanding officers. For example, he bestowed fulsome praise on General Sir John Doyle:

> General Doyle was a true, hearty Irishman and well fitted to have command of men. He had none of that pride and sullenness which too often attend those in authority. He was ever attentive to our wants and his affability and kindness can never be forgotten by any soldier in the brigade. The men that mounted his guard seldom went without a glass of rum in the morning from his own hand.[2]

On one occasion Doyle personally dealt with the commissary to obtain bread and rum for the men of his brigade.

By contrast, Colonel Spencer, who took temporary command of the brigade on the march back from Cairo, earned Nicol's sharp criticism. General Hutchinson had arranged for camels to transport the men's packs

> but Colonel Spencer said there was no need for this. This officer had had command of the brigade since General Doyle left and what different treatment we received, the one always looking out for the comfort of the soldiers, the other harassing us as far as he thought we would bear it.[3]

These comments, combined with the respect for Abercromby and the frequent, concerned references to Sir John Moore, who was with the expedition and whom Nicol knew well from previous service, demonstrate the qualities valued by soldiers in their commanding officers. Above all, the men recognised genuine concern for their wellbeing.

Immediate circumstances in Egypt were uncomfortable. Although initially they were troubled by heavy dews at night and showers of rain and hail, these soon gave way to excessive heat and extreme thirst: ' ... in this dry sand, with a burning sun overhead and living on salt provisions, water is a precious article indeed.' The water of the Nile

> is the only good water in the country [despite being very muddy] and is even said to be nourishing for the body. I have known

some of our own men drink from ten to twelve quarts of it in the course of a day's march, just as it was lifted out of the river and never heard that it hurt anyone.[4]

On one occasion Nicol sat by a well and drank as if he would never be satisfied.

The heat was a constant problem, made even worse by the effects of the sirocco:

We had one day's hot wind from the south which will ever be remarkable to the Egyptian army. The morning was lowering and the sun was of a blood red colour. It began to blow at 9 o'clock: and woe be to him that is from shelter, as neither man nor beast can survive in it three days. It came from the desert as hot as the opening of an oven door, bringing small sand like mist along with it. All our sentinels were called in and the cattle crept close to the ground for fear. The buffaloes took to the river, covering themselves all but the nose in the water; flesh putrefied; any metal substance could not be touched with the naked hand; and no man was able to stir out of his tent until the evening when happily the wind changed to the north-west.[5]

Nor was marching easy. On 17 May occurred

the worst day's march we had in the country. Very few men had had time to get water in their canteens, at every step we sank over the ankles in light sand, and for three paces to the front we slipped one back. Hundreds of our people dropped down and had to be taken up by the camels[6]

whereupon they risked being killed for their arms and accoutrements by the Bedouin Arabs.

Food was never such a problem. Initially a market was established at Aboukir where food was plentiful and cheap, and much more acceptable than the quartermaster's salt beef and pork, to which the men were even invited to help themselves just to get rid of it. The good supply of fresh food continued at nearly every place they passed through. At a dirty village called Itko, for example, 'The inhabitants came among us in a friendly manner selling bread, fried fish, eggs, fruit etc. We found good water here and the Arabs came round with it in skins selling it to us.'[7]

31

Nicol was an educated young man and keenly aware of the Biblical and historical connotations of Egypt:

> We were now upon Scripture ground; we had come from a distant island in the sea to the country of the proud Pharaohs to carry on war where Nebuchadnezzar and Alexander the Great, Caesar, and other great warriors had put armies in motion.[8]

Particularly apparent were the 'plagues' of Egypt:

> This part of the country so abounded in frogs that it was impossible to get at the water in the river without treading on them, and from their slimy nature many a tumble some of our men got: after dark they croaked so as to be heard at a considerable distance from the river ... The flies are in swarms about the towns; you must keep your hands in motion to prevent them going down your throat or into your eyes. In some places the ground was black with fleas ... As for sand lice ... I have seen so many in the hearts [of date trees] that they might have been gathered in handfuls.
>
> One day locusts passed from west to east in such numbers as to darken the air.

As Nicol commented, 'Some of the plagues of Moses exist here yet.'[9]

There were plagues of a different kind, including the bubonic plague itself, which appeared in the army within a fortnight of the landing, in the general hospital converted from the French barracks at Aboukir. Nicol was sent there with a burial party, to bury a surgeon and two women in one hole and seven men in another, all victims of the plague. Nicol also referred to an eye condition that led to seriously impaired sight or blindness. Often a fully-sighted man would be paired with one suffering from this condition, one to watch and one to listen. This affliction was ophthalmia, endemic in Egypt and caused by the same bacterium as chlamydia. It was so contagious that it became the scourge of the army for the next few decades. Then there were the boils and prickly heat; few of the army that marched to Cairo escaped these afflictions.

On a more positive note, Nicol was interested in everything he saw. Not surprisingly, he visited the Great Pyramid at Giza where, in the worst tourist fashion, he 'wrought very hard and got D.NICOL, 92 REGT carved, and broke my knife while finishing the job; this is on the south-east corner, and is likely to stand some time.'[10] He also

The Pyramids. (*Author's collection*)

visited mosques, a school, where he demonstrated the European way of writing to the teacher in return for his civility in explaining what was going on, and a weaver's shop. Perhaps by this Nicol exemplifies how an intelligent soldier (of whom there were not a few in the army) responded to new experiences and alien situations.

After the breakdown of the Peace of Amiens in 1803 the 92nd saw action in Denmark (1807) and were then sent to the Peninsula. The largest part of the regiment was with Sir John Moore during the campaign of 1808 which ended in the retreat to Corunna. Nicol, however, was left behind in Lisbon, having developed a fever which incapacitated him for two months. When Sir Arthur Wellesley returned to Portugal in 1809 the recovered invalids of the 92nd were formed into a company in a battalion of detachments. They were involved in the crossing of the Douro (May 1809) which drove the French under Marshal Soult out of Portugal. Wellesley then took his army into Spain to act with a Spanish army. This culminated in the battle of Talavera on 27 and 28 July.

The battalion of detachments conducted itself well during the battle but on the second day at about four o'clock Nicol was struck by a musket ball, which grazed his left knee and passed through his right leg about 2 inches below the kneecap.

Although victorious, Wellesley made a tactical withdrawal to Portugal four days after the battle. Nicol's leg was too swollen for marching and he had to remain in Talavera with the other wounded.

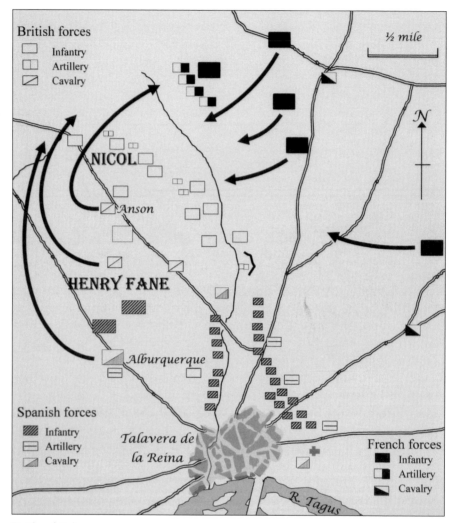

Battle of Talavera.

Two days later, as the French advanced on the town, the Spanish also departed, taking their wounded with them but leaving the British behind. These men were now in a sorry state, obliged to dress each other's wounds and knowing that they were about to become prisoners of war.

In Egypt Nicol often commented on the bonhomie that developed between British and French soldiers whenever they were not actually fighting each other. This pertained after the French arrived in

Battle of Talavera. (*Author's collection*)

Talavera. The French plundered but they made sure the British had some of the food they found.

Nevertheless, Nicol's situation was grave. The swelling increased. There was talk of amputation. Nicol resisted, saying that he might as well go to the grave with two legs as one. Then a bizarre incident occurred:

> One night after it was dark a French drummer was pursuing a woman belonging to the Twenty-Fourth Regiment in full flight along the passage, when she fell right on my wounded leg. I roared out, the woman shrieked, and the drummer, thinking he was to be attacked, drew his sword and went off cursing. I was in great distress and a high fever all night; but next morning, on dressing my wound, seven small pieces of bone came out of it, some of them about the size of the teeth of a dressing-comb, and a piece of my trousers that had been driven in by the ball. From this time I mended every day.[11]

The French continued to treat the prisoners well. Marshal Mortier visited them, to apologise that it was not in his power to supply them with the things they needed but while bread was to be got for his own troops the wounded prisoners should be first served. He also pointed out that the French were treating them better than their own side, since the Spanish could have transported them to safety.

There were many notable acts of kindness during the long journey to the prison depot at Briançon, in the French Alps. On one occasion Nicol begged a French soldier to sell him some food. The man refused but said he would give it to him for 'l'amor de Dieu'. Wherever they passed, the local inhabitants also gave them food or money. Even an Irish captain who had been 'out' during the rebellion gave him a dollar for wine. Indeed, the only harshness Nicol experienced was from a gendarme who lost some prisoners and vented his frustration on the rest of his charges.

Nicol arrived at Briançon on 21 June 1810 and was appalled by what he saw in the grand square, where about 1,000 British prisoners were assembled in a miserable condition, inadequately clothed in pieces of old blanket. 'A cold shudder came over me as I looked at them. Their condition was a disgrace to the French nation because there was an abundance of clothing in the stores.'[12]

The prisoners were accommodated in bombproof barracks where they were organised into messes of thirty-three men, three messes constituting a company with a 'chief of division' in charge. As a French-speaker Nicol was appointed chief of division. This granted him more liberty but also required him to make out returns for provisions and mess utensils, and compile sick reports.

Food was not plentiful:

12 oz of bread and 6 oz of beef, with a very small allowance of rice or callarences [fresh food i.e. vegetables], which were barely sufficient to support nature; we were allowed one sou and a half a day from the French, paid monthly and two sous per day from Lloyd's Committee. What bedding we had was rotten and full of vermin, from which we could not keep ourselves free.[13]

Extra provisions could be bought but the allowance was not sufficient to purchase much. Nicol, therefore, wrote letters to Colonel Gordon at Lyons (who sent the six men of the 92nd three francs apiece) and Sir John Hope, the colonel of the regiment. As a result, Nicol and the others received their Danish prize money, fifty-three francs each, and back pay of forty-nine francs, as well as getting their pay every month thereafter. No wonder Nicol's colleagues of the 92nd celebrated his thirty-third birthday in good style.

Nicol seems to have been more stoical about imprisonment than many of his colleagues. He made no attempt to escape and, although tempted for a moment, resisted the cajolery of a Captain Reilly of the Irish brigade (made up of Irish emigrants and prisoners of war) to enlist in French service. When a much discussed exchange failed, some men were in tears and others were struck dumb. Nicol sympathised, but chose to get on with his life.

He coped by following a timetable. After a harsh winter

> I began my walks in the square from six to eight every morning weather permitting, then went in, took a little breakfast. And read or wrote till dinner was ready, then kept talking or hearing stories, news, etc, until afternoon when I walked for an hour in the square before we were locked up, which was always about sunset. This I carried on day after day.[14]

He also leased some waste land which had been turned into gardens. Here he built a shelter of stones which became the headquarters of the 92nd regiment and also his refuge where he wrote his memoirs up to that point. He tried to grow crops, but nothing came to maturity. Nevertheless, it kept him busy.

On 29 December 1813 Nicol finally left Briançon. The prisoners were marched north to Lyons and on to Dijon. France was under attack from the south and the east, so the prisoners were taken further north and then west to Normandy, finishing up in Brittany. On 4 April they were told secretly that Paris had fallen. Six days later the Bourbon white cockade made its first appearance in Rennes and the prisoners reciprocated by hoisting a sheet as a white flag. Napoleon's reign was over – for a year. The exchange of prisoners began almost at once. Nicol finally reached England on 22 May, landing at Plymouth.

Not surprisingly he was now retired, 'worn out'. When Napoleon returned from Elba Nicol briefly joined a veteran battalion but after Waterloo he retired for good. He survived until October 1851, dying of an inflammation of the lungs. Until the last few months of his life he was employed by the various companies that published the works of Sir Walter Scott, and seems to have been an ideal employee just as he had been a model soldier.

Researching Daniel Nicol

Daniel Nicol's memoirs of his twenty years of service with the 92nd, Gordon Highlanders, were first published in 1911 by Mackenzie Macbride along with some other documents, the whole collection entitled *With Napoleon at Waterloo*. (Nicol's part of the text was reprinted by Leonaur Books in 2007.) As with all memoirs, there is the possibility of distortion caused by hindsight, but Nicol was writing before the 'Great War' was over. Indeed, parts of the text are contemporaneous. Furthermore, the muster rolls for the 92nd (WO12) support in detail the story he tells, and his discharge papers (WO97) give as the reason for discharge 'wound in the right leg', the wound he received at Talavera. As for his experiences in Egypt, these match other accounts, particularly that of his fellow Gordon Highlander, Duncan Robertson. Obviously, even if a researcher is fortunate enough to come across written evidence in the form of letters, journals or memoirs, the contents should always be checked against military records, particularly in the case of memoirs written years after the event.

And there are problems with Daniel Nicol, starting with the spelling of his name. In the General Service Medal Roll, where he is listed as receiving bars for Egypt and Talavera, as might be expected from his memoirs, his surname is spelt Nicholl. Such variant spellings always need to be considered because clerks often wrote down what they heard, a point demonstrated by those British surnames which have a clutch of different versions.

Furthermore, although the published version of his memoirs describes him as Sergeant Nicol, neither the muster rolls nor his discharge papers give him this rank. He was a corporal while in Egypt, as the muster rolls reveal, but at no point did he rise to sergeant. There are two possible explanations, though, to explain the discrepancy. It could be an acknowledgement of his function as *chef de bataillon* while in Briançon. On the other hand, after he had spent a year in a veteran battalion, he was invited to return to his regiment with the rank of sergeant, an offer he declined.

Most problematic, though, are the biographical details that Macbride included in his introduction to the memoirs, or diary as he called it, and the information on the discharge papers. Macbride took his information from Nicol's own account. There is no reason to question whether a 15-year-old lad would run away to the Army; it happened often enough. The discharge papers, however, state that Nicol was a 20-year-old labourer when he enlisted on 13 March 1794, and was born in the parish of Greyfriars, Edinburgh. Obviously, some further evidence is required. The 1851 census, taken months before Nicol died, supports his own version of events in respect of age and birthplace, which suggests that a well-educated 15-year-old desperate to disappear and, being quite well-grown (he was 5' 7" tall), added a few years to make himself acceptable to the Army.

Notes

1. Daniel Nicol, *Sergeant Nicol, The Experiences of a Gordon Highlander during the Napoleonic Wars in Egypt, the Peninsula & France*, p. 50.
2. Ibid., p. 58.
3. Ibid., p. 80.
4. Ibid., p. 59.
5. Ibid., p. 70.
6. Ibid., p. 69.
7. Ibid., pp. 56–7.
8. Ibid., p. 45.
9. Ibid., pp. 71–2.
10. Ibid., p. 76.
11. Ibid., p. 115.
12. Ibid., p. 142.
13. Ibid., p. 143.
14. Ibid., p. 146.

Chapter Three

LETTERS HOME
William Wheeler of the 51st

When William Wheeler, a 24-year-old labourer from Bath, joined the 2nd Royal Surrey Militia in 1808, he not only embarked on a career as a soldier which would last until 1825 but also began a habit of writing letters to his mother for the interest of his family. Wheeler himself preserved these letters when he discovered that they had been kept, thus saving for posterity one of the most engaging collections of accounts, anecdotes and reflections on a soldier's life during the Napoleonic Wars. Above all else, their sense of immediacy gives them a veracity which few memoirs, written retrospectively, can match.

Wheeler did not remain long in the Militia. In April 1809 he took the opportunity to transfer into the regular army, initially signing on for seven years, although this became 'for life' in 1816. 'I have at length escaped from the Militia without being flead alive,' he explained. 'I made up my mind to volunteer but into what regiment I cared not a straw, so I determined to go with the greatest number.'[1] His decision took him into the 51st, Yorkshire West Riding, with 127 of his fellows, rejoicing that he had 'escaped from the one I left with a whole skin'.[2]

When Wheeler joined the regiment its strength had been depleted by the rigours of the retreat to Corunna. Nevertheless, within months he found himself on the way to Walcheren, the 51st being part of an expedition to seize Antwerp from the French. Despite some initial success, this expedition ended in muddle and failure. Wheeler saw action, however, and was much struck by the aftermath of battle:

the dead and dying laying about covered with blood, sweat, and dust looks frightful, the wounded some in their last agony begging for water, others writhing under pain, calling on some one to shoot them. But amidst all this pain and misery, it is

British Redcoats. (*Philip Haythornthwaite*)

delightful to see the very same soldiers, who an hour before were dealing destruction about them, tendering all the assistance in their power to a fallen enemy.[3]

Wheeler never lost either his sympathy for the sufferings of both friend and enemy, or his admiration for human endurance.

The 51st returned to England in September 1809 much weakened by 'a severe ague', a malarial fever which affected all the Walcheren regiments.

41

The Iberian Peninsula.

In March 1811 they arrived in Portugal to join Wellington in his campaign against Marshal Masséna. The French were driven back to Spain and Wheeler fought his first pitched battle at Fuentes de Oñoro. On 5 May, the third day of this protracted affair, the 51st came under fierce French attack:

> Thanks to Colonel M[ainwaring] we came off safe, although the shot was flying pretty thick, yet his superior skill baffled all the efforts of the enemy, he took advantage of the ground and led us out of a scrape without loss. I shall never forget him, he dismounted off his horse, faced us and frequently called the time 'right, left' as he was accustomed to when drilling the regiment.[4]

Mainwaring's words to his battalion, as he walked backwards to face his men were: 'Keep in step and they shall not defeat us.' When a shot passed under his horse's belly, so that the unfortunate animal reared up in alarm, Mainwaring immediately declared that it would get no rations that night for its cowardice.

The 'scrape' Wheeler referred to was caused by Wellington extending his right to the point where it became vulnerable to French

The position of the 7th division at Fuentes de Oñoro.

cavalry. The newly-formed 7th division, to which the 51st belonged, was saved by its calmness under fire, and the combined efforts of the light division, the allied cavalry and Norman Ramsey with his two guns of the Royal Horse Artillery.

While Wellington was operating in the north, with Almeida as his objective, Marshal Beresford was besieging Badajoz further south. The first siege had to be raised when Marshal Soult brought a relieving force from Andalusia. After the bloody battle of Albuera, Wellington marched south with the 7th division as part of his force and renewed the siege. Wheeler's reaction to being winded by round shot is revealing of his character:

> One of the round shot must have passed pretty near my cranium, I thought I was wounded, my head ached violently. I felt the pain a long time and it was with difficulty I could perform my

duty. Had I been working in a place where there was no danger I certainly should have given up, but here I was ashamed to complain, lest any of my comrades should laugh at me.[5]

Wheeler twice volunteered for the storming party, consciously putting his life at extra risk. On the second occasion he avoided being taken prisoner by using his ingenuity. The order was given to retire but he, with eight or nine others, found himself cut off by the French:

> I hit upon an expedient that answered well. I threw myself down by a man who was shot through the head and daubed my white haversack with his blood. I shewed this to the enemy when they ordered me to get up and go into the fort. From the appearance of the blood they must have thought I had a very bad wound in the hip, so they all left me.[6]

The siege was raised for a second time and the rest of 1811 was spent on the Spanish-Portuguese border. In 1812, though, Wellington took the war into Spain. Having captured Ciudad Rodrigo on 19 January and Badajoz, at last, on 6 April, he then advanced on Salamanca. After some protracted manoeuvring the French, under Marshal Marmont, were defeated on 18 July. From Salamanca the allied army advanced to Madrid and a rapturous welcome:

> I never before witnessed such a scene ... the people were mad with joy. They called us 'their deliverers, their saviours.' And by a thousand other names ... the air was rent with the deafening shouts of 'Vivi Wellington, Vivi les Angolese, Vivi les Ilandos' and by ten thousand other Vivis.[7]

This euphoria, which infected the soldiers as well as the people of Madrid, was dissipated by the subsequent failure to take Burgos and the horrors of the retreat which followed:

> The fatigue and distress of this retreat will long be remembered by those who shared in it ... Our camp or resting place would soon be reduced to mud, ankle deep, on which we must lie or sit for the night. Our blankets were so wet that each morning before we could put them into our knapsacks they were obliged to be wrung. The roads were so cut up that it was with the greatest difficulty the hardiest soldiers could march. Provisions were scarce, shoes failed and many were barefoot.[8]

But according to Wheeler, the soldiers' only complaint was that they were denied the chance to fight the French.

Although 1812 ended with the army back where it started, in Portugal, the next year saw Wellington drive the French over the Pyrenees. Victory at Vitoria (18 June), when Wheeler claimed his fair share of the loot left on the battlefield, was followed by a succession of fierce actions in the mountains, as well as the fall of San Sebastian and Pamplona. The French then took up a strong position on the Nivelle which Wellington broke through on 10 November. For Wheeler, this action nearly brought about the end of his military career:

> ... as I was in the act of pulling my trigger I received a wound in both legs, the ball glanced or scraped the skin just above the outside ankle of the left foot and passed through the gristle behind the ankle of the right just missing the bone.[9]

Soldiers marching. (*National Army Museum*)

There followed a long period in hospital, including five weeks in the 'incurable ward' after his wound sloughed, probably as a result of the dead skin caused by extensive bruising. His condition worsened despite 'all the remedies applied to prevent mortification ... the wounded part and the foot were swollen to an enormous size, and the wound was as large over as a tea saucer'. Twice he was prepared for amputation but

> the little Spanish doctor who had charge of me overruled it ... He brought from his home a small bottle filled with some thing like pepper and salt mixed, with this he covered the wound on which he put lint, bandaged it up, crossed himself, muttered something to himself and left me.[10]

Whatever the mixture, it saved Wheeler's leg and possibly his life.

Safely recovered, he sent his family a harrowing picture of the incurable ward:

> one continued scene of misery and woe the dreadful suffering of the patients is beyond description. During the five weeks I was in it, what numbers have I seen die under the most writhing torture, and their places filled again by others, who only come to pass a few days in misery, and then to be taken to their last home.

Wheeler also noted that there was 'No minister of religion to cheer the dying sinner'. There were chaplains with the army, but 'If these Reverend Gentlemen were stationed at the sick depots and made to attend to the hospitals, they would be much more usefully employed than following the army with their brace of dogs and gun.'[11]

Despite his fears that he would never walk again without a stick, he eventually recovered and was with the 51st at Waterloo, by this time with the rank of sergeant. Although posted near Hougoumont, scene of fierce fighting, the 51st took relatively light casualties. They then formed part of the army of occupation in France until the end of 1815. Later they were posted to the Ionian Islands, a British protectorate at the time. There was no further action and Wheeler spent his last few years with the regiment as schoolmaster sergeant. He was invalided out, aged 43 on 21 May 1828, with a pension of 1/10d a day.

So much for what he did. What about the man himself? In January 1813 Wheeler wrote:

> We have spent a very comfortable Christmas, you know I am one of these sort of mortals that do not stand to niceties. Youth and

health with a moderate share of the good things of this world always satisfies me. I have often spent many happy hours, when on the outlying picket, when sitting by the fire smoking my pipe and listening to the marvellous tales of my comrades.[12]

A good supply of food, good, cheap wine, and plenty of tobacco made him a contented man.

On another occasion he showed some impatience for action. 'The sooner the campaign opens the better. It is true we shall have to encounter great dangers and fatigues. What of that, it is the very life and soul of a soldier.'[13] In other words, he was the epitome of the stoical British soldier.

He did, however, possess a keen sense of justice. A sergeant and corporal of the regiment were tried for passing a drunken man for guard (even though he was not drunk at the time). They were sentenced to be reduced to the ranks and to receive 300 lashes. Wheeler commented: 'Here you see the Earl of Dalhousie ordering a Court Martial, himself or some of his staff witnesses, then he approves of the finding of the court and sees the sentences carried into execution.'[14] When a sergeant with an exemplary career was ordered to be shot for striking an officer under severe provocation, Wheeler could not contain his sense of outrage. His final comment, 'let us hope he has obtained that mercy in another world that was denied him in this', makes his feelings clear. He might recognise the need for discipline; he certainly had no sympathy for the drunken private, mentioned above, who received 500 lashes; but he believed in fairness above all else.

One quality Wheeler lacked was ambition. His mother wondered why he had not sought promotion. He explained that he could have been a sergeant, but he did not want the responsibility. It was enough to do his duty and keep out of trouble. Six months later, however, and against his better judgement, he was promoted to corporal. 'Our Paymaster recommended me to set the [company] books to right' after the pay sergeant was killed. The Adjutant then decided that 'I should have my choice of two things, that was, I should be put in orders that day for Corporal, and I might do the duty, either with, or without pay.'[15] It was a simple choice.

We may wonder that a man who was described on his discharge papers as a labourer had clerical skills, which are referred to on more than one occasion. He was well-read, however. The letters contain frequent quotations from and allusions to Shakespeare plays, as well as quotations from *Tristram Shandy* and the moralising letters of Lord Chesterfield. He was also familiar with the *Odyssey*. His liking for books becomes apparent after the fall of the Retiro forts in Madrid:

> I strolled into the summer house and was agreeably surprised to find a quantity of books, Spanish, French and English. I secured all I could find in my own tongue but as I have not the means of carrying them I distributed them amongst my comrades whom I know are fond of reading.[16]

Not quite the conventional view of the British soldier at this time.

Wheeler's thoughts on the foreign units that served in the 7th division are interesting and probably typical of British soldiers. The division was known as The Mongrels because of its British, French, German and Portuguese composition. The Chasseurs Britannique, for example,

> was originally formed of French loyalists, but the old hands are continually dropping off and they are replaced by volunteers from the French prisons. A great number of these men enter our service for no other purpose than to go over to their army as soon as an opportunity offers (and who can blame them). The consequence is the major part of the Corps cannot be trusted. I wish they were at the Devil or any where else, so that we were not plagued with them, for we are obliged to perform all the most dangerous and fatiguing duty of the campaign – for if these men were intrusted on the out posts, more would desert than they do at present.[17]

Strictly disciplined by their French émigré officers, however, they performed well under fire, as Wheeler acknowledged on several occasions, although their polyglot composition could cause confusion:

> About midnight when all were fast asleep some one called out 'The enemy, the enemy, Fall in!' You can easily conceive what a confused scene followed, the place was as dark as possible, as full as it would hold of soldiers laying down fully accoutered with their firelocks between their legs. All were up in a moment, shouting out 'Where are they, where is the door, fix your bayonets', some were cursing and swearing. The C. Britannique

Regt., comprised of men from every country in Europe, were each calling out in their own native tongue. Add to this the noise occasioned by fixing bayonets. Everyone of course were seeking the door but no one could find it, at length some got out and discovered it was a false alarm.[18]

As for the Germans, Wheeler shared the general respect for the King's German Legion, even though the original cadre of Hanoverian soldiers had been diluted by the admission of German prisoners of war. The Black Brunswickers ('The Duke of Brunswicker's Oels', as Wheeler called them) were a different matter, almost as bad as the Chasseurs Britannique. Too many of them came from the prisoner of war camps. He described how two men deserted from Campo Mayor and another three were shot for desertion. Wheeler reported their execution dispassionately, although he was obviously shocked by the mangled remains.

As we have seen, Wheeler congratulated himself on escaping from the Militia without being flogged. This fear was provoked by serving under Major Hudson,

as great a tyrant as ever disgraced the army. This man delighted in torturing the men, every man in the corps hated him, when once a soldier came under his lash it was no use for any officer to plead for him. If he was young, his reply was: 'It will do him good, make him grow and make him know better for the future.' On the other hand if he was getting on in years, the brute would say, 'Oh, he is old enough to know better.'[19]

He was quick to recognise a good commanding officer, however. Colonel Mainwaring, an eccentric Irishman of uncertain temper, was in command of the 51st when Wheeler joined. He could show great generosity but was subject to 'fits of passion [which] would lead or drive him into acts of violence that I'm sure must give him pain when his better judgement had resumed her proper seat'. Yet on one occasion he spared three men the lash because he refused to be the man who broke their backs: '. . . if at times he was driven to excess by passion, he was in the whole a humane man. I hope his successor will not turn out worse.'[20]

That successor, Colonel Mitchell, figures frequently in the letters without attracting any comment on his character. In March 1813 he returned to England on leave, and command passed to Major Roberts, who had lost a hand during the retreat to Corunna:

> He is reported to be a lion in the field. This is the first time I ever saw him, his having been employed on the staff at Bristol. I do not know what to make of him. He seems very fond of using the cats, and if he continues as he has begun it will not be long before everyone will get a taste.[21]

Wheeler quickly changed his opinion, describing Roberts as the best commander the regiment could have. When he was wounded and invalided home, Wheeler wrote that they had lost in him a good, kind, brave and generous officer.

Like most men in the ranks, Wheeler appreciated the good officers, of whatever rank. His eulogy of Captain Douglas, killed in the Pyrenees, sums up his opinion:

> ... *he* stood high as a brave soldier, but he was in possession of another virtue, rarely to be met with to so great a degree in any man – it was a noble generosity and good will that he extended to all about him ... he never had any trouble in keeping his men in order, as a look or a word from him had more effect than 500 lashes would from some officers. Our regret for his loss can be much easier imagined than described.[22]

To conclude on a lighter note, Wheeler's letters are full of anecdotes designed to entertain his family. To take just one example, while he was on outpost duty, close to the enemy lines:

> The officer commanding our piquet asked me if I had any objection to take charge of the outpost the last hour before daylight as he considered the duty too hard for the Corporals, who besides performing this duty had to plant the other sentries. To be selected for this post roused my ambition and I accepted the proposal with delight. When I got to my post, the Corporal pointed to two figures about the common height of men, and in a direct line to the spot occupied by the enemy's advance, and about half-way between us. He said they had been walking about all the time he was posted, did not know what to make of them, etc. He then crawled back to the piquet leaving us to keep a sharp lookout on the two strange gentlemen, who kept walking about. Sometimes they seemed almost close to us then, as if

doubtful, they would retire. We were ready cocked but they might be deserters, besides to fire on two when there were three of us would not look well, and it would perhaps set both sides a popping and create an unnecessary alarm.

At length daylight shewed us who these two gentlemen were. It was nothing but two bushes, now and then bending up and down by the wind that ever and anon swept through the valley. It was now time to crawl back, we found the Corporal had made his report of the two strangers and that the whole piquet was on the alert. When I unravelled the mystery, it caused a hearty laugh.[23]

... and one can almost hear Wheeler joining in.

Researching William Wheeler

The joy of William Wheeler's letters (first published in 1951, edited by B.H. Liddell Hart and subsequently reprinted) is their unselfconscious character. He was not writing for posterity or even to inform the public, as would some later memoirists. His letters were a spontaneous response to what was happening around him and designed to enable his family to understand the day-to-day experiences of a soldier's life, amplified by the thoughts and feelings of the moment. This gives them immediacy and veracity.

Wheeler's military career can be followed from its beginnings in the muster rolls of the Surrey Militia (WO13 – militia and volunteers) and the 51st Foot (WO12). Because he survived to claim a pension, the appropriate document in WO97 (which can be found on Find My Past) gives Bath as his place of birth and 25 as his age upon enlistment in the 51st. In theory this should make finding the record of his birth fairly simple, but no William Wheeler of the right age has been found in the parish records. This search, incidentally, was kindly undertaken by a local archivist. There is a William Wheeler born in nearby Wiltshire who would fit, and it is possible that the family moved to Bath when William was a small child, so that he later gave Bath as his place of birth. A search for the parents of this William Wheeler might provide information one way or the other.

The discharge papers also give a digest of his promotions. After four years 174 days he was promoted to corporal, reluctantly, as his letters make clear. He was a corporal for a year 154 days, quite a short period, and then spent thirteen years ninety-four days as a sergeant,

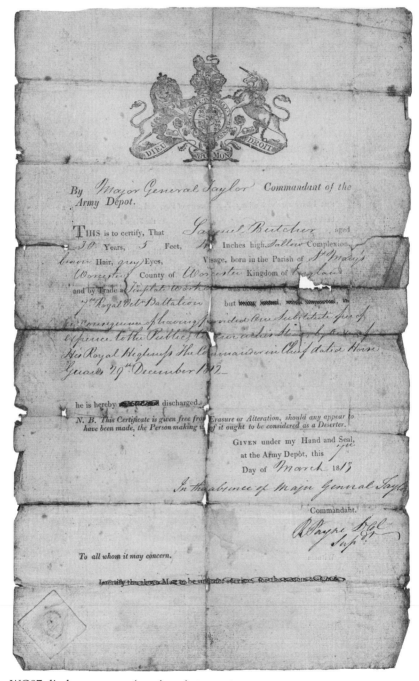

WO97 discharge paper (specimen). (*National Army Museum*)

which suggests that the regiment valued him rather more highly than he valued himself.

As with all discharge papers there is the description designed to prevent fraud; in Wheeler's case: height 5′9″, dark hair, hazel eyes and a dark complexion. This last may have been the result of the years he spent in hot climates.

Wheeler survived for twenty-three years after his discharge from the army, and is recorded in the 1851 census. Of course, William Wheeler is not a particularly unusual name but the letters tell us that our William Wheeler had a wife called Priscilla, as does the William Wheeler living in Caroline Place, Walcott, Bath. He also had a daughter, Angelina, and a son, Edwin. By 1851 Wheeler was in his sixties. He was still drawing his pension from Chelsea, but he was also working as a porter to the Walcott commissioners, a position his son later inherited.

One further point of interest concerns his daughter. She had a Wesleyan baptism at Holsworthy, Devon, in November 1833 when her parents were living at Morwenstowe in Cornwall. This may explain the absence of a record of William and Priscilla's marriage in the parish record of Plymouth, where they married. Methodist records can be accessed on http//freepage.genealogy.rootsweb. ancestry.com. Angelina's Methodist baptism certainly indicates that either William or Priscilla was Methodist.

Notes

1. *The Letters of Private Wheeler*, p. 17.
2. Ibid., p. 19.
3. Ibid., p. 31.
4. Ibid., p. 55.
5. Ibid., p. 58.
6. Ibid., p. 62.
7. Ibid., pp. 90–1.
8. Ibid., p. 102.
9. Ibid., p. 135.
10. Ibid., p. 152.
11. Ibid., p. 153.
12. Ibid., p. 105.
13. Ibid., p. 78.
14. Ibid., p. 109.
15. Ibid., p. 134.
16. Ibid., p. 94.
17. Ibid., p. 67.

18. Ibid., p. 99.
19. Ibid., p. 15.
20. Ibid., pp. 70–1.
21. Ibid., p. 106.
22. Ibid., p. 128.
23. Ibid., p. 130.

Chapter Four

FIRST IN AND LAST OUT
Harris, Costello and Plunket of the
95th Rifles

Imagine an old shoemaker sitting in his shop in a narrow London street. He probably has the vacant look of a man who gazes on things unseen, his memories of many years before when he was young and fit and wore the dark green uniform of a regiment that considered itself the elite of the British infantry. He reminisces of times past, of the battlefields of the Peninsula and, most vividly of all, of 'comrades, long mouldered to dust, once again performing the acts of heroes'.[1]

The shoemaker, a shepherd's son from Dorset, has been persuaded to think back more than twenty years; to share his most treasured memories with an eager listener who will one day publish them as *The Recollections of Rifleman Harris* ...

Benjamin Harris, like William Wheeler, was balloted into the army. Unlike Wheeler, he was sent not to the Militia but to the Army of Reserve, a means used by the government in 1803 to boost army numbers after the collapse of the Peace of Amiens. He was 22 when he joined the 66th Foot. Men from the Army of Reserve were encouraged to enlist for general service, otherwise they could not serve outside the British Isles but Harris chose not to accept the king's shilling.

Harris went with his regiment to Ireland, where soldiers were principally engaged in recruiting and performing police and customs duties. He was in the light company, 'being smart and active'. Light infantry was becoming increasingly important tactically and in 1804 the light company of the 66th joined with other light companies in Dublin to receive special training. Here Harris saw the 95th for the first time and immediately fell in love with their dashing appearance. Two years later he was in Cashel when he encountered a recruiting

95th Rifleman. (*Philip Haythornthwaite*)

party of the 95th and enlisted into the second battalion. This was possible because he had not signed up for general service.

Recruiting was very much a matter of drink and jollity. Harris now found himself with volunteers from the Irish Militia,

the most reckless and devil-may-care set of men I ever beheld before or since. Being joined by a sergeant of the 92nd Highlanders, and a Highland piper of the same regiment – a pair of real rollicking blades – I thought we would all go mad together ... on arriving at Clonmel we were as glorious as any soldiers in all Christendom would wish to be.[2]

The drinking and high spirits continued throughout the march to Ashford, Kent, regularly punctuated by spats between the Catholics and Protestants of the party which Harris, as the only Englishman, could view with dispassionate amusement.

During the summer of 1807 Harris experienced active service in neutral Denmark. The objective of the expedition was to seize the Danish fleet at Copenhagen before it fell into French hands. Five companies from the 1/95th and five from the 2/95th were in Major-General Sir Arthur Wellesley's brigade. At Køge on 26 August the brigade easily routed a volunteer Danish force; poor preparation for what lay ahead at the other end of Europe. Copenhagen was shelled into surrender, the Danish ships were secured and the campaign was over. On 16 November the ten Rifle companies landed at Deal.

In the Iberian Peninsula, however, events were developing dramatically. The Portuguese refused to accept the Continental System and Napoleon responded by sending Marshal Junot to invade the country with tacit Spanish support. The following spring Napoleon settled the internecine quarrels of the Spanish royal family by placing his elder brother, Joseph, on the Spanish throne. Both countries now appealed for British aid.

Like Nicol of the 92nd, Harris found himself part of a force assembled under Sir Arthur Wellesley at Cork. Originally intended for service in South America, the expedition was diverted to Portugal, landing at Mondego Bay on 1 August. 'The Rifles were the first out of the vessels because we were always in the front of the advance and in the rear of the retreat.'[3]

Harris was immediately struck by the heat:

With a burning sun above our heads, and our feet sinking at every step into the hot sand, we soon began to feel the misery of

95th Riflemen skirmishing. *(Philip Haythornthwaite)*

the frightful load we were condemned to march and fight under. The weight I myself toiled under was tremendous, and I often wonder at the strength I possessed that enabled me to endure it.[4]

The load he carried included his haversack, blanket, greatcoat, rifle and pouch, with eighty rounds of ball cartridge, and all his shoe-making equipment.

After a skirmish at Obidos, where the first man hit was Lieutenant Bunbury of the 95th, the British then came up against a French force under General Delaborde at Roliça on 17 August. The enemy had taken position on high ground which presented a difficult challenge for the attacking army. Harris described the riflemen's skirmishing tactics:

we advanced pretty close upon the enemy. I took advantage of whatever cover I could find, throwing myself down behind a small bank where I lay so secure that, although the Frenchmen's bullets fell pretty thickly around, I was able to knock several over without being dislodged. Whilst lying in this spot I fired away every round I had in my pouch.[5]

From his vantage point Harris witnessed the near annihilation of the 29th and the death of their colonel. The 95th were also taking casualties:

> We had caught it pretty handsomely too, for there was no cover for us, and we were rather too near ... 'Fire and retire' is a very good sound, but the Rifles were not over-fond of such notes. We never performed that manoeuvre unless it was made pretty plain to us that it was necessary.[6]

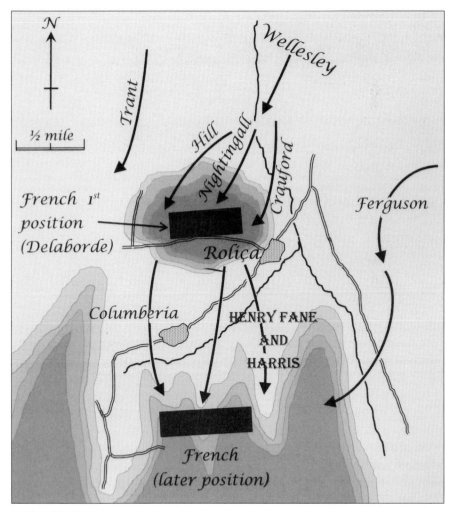

Battle of Roliça.

Battle of Roliça. *(Author's collection)*

General Hill, 'Daddy' Hill to the troops, restored the 29th to order and brought them up to the charge. Almost at the same moment Harris suffered the harrowing experience of helplessly watching a comrade die. Sergeant Alexander Fraser took a musket ball in the abdomen. 'Froth came from his mouth, and perspiration poured from his face ... I think that poor fellow suffered more the short time he was dying than any man I saw in the same circumstances.' But 'The sight of such bloodshed will not suffer the mind to dwell on any particular casualty, even though it be one's dearest friend.'[7]

Eventually, the outnumbered French were forced to retreat. Roliça, however, was merely a prelude to the more significant action at Vimeiro four days later when the British, with some Portuguese support, found themselves faced with a larger French force under Marshal Junot. British reinforcements had been landed since Roliça, so Wellesley still enjoyed a numerical advantage, although outmatched in cavalry and guns. Harris surveyed the scene as the British waited for the first French attack:

Our lines glittered with bright arms, and the features of the men were stern as they stood with their eyes fixed unalterably upon the enemy. The proud colours of England floated over the heads of the different battalions, and the dark cannon on the rising ground were all in readiness to commence the awful work of death with a noise that would deafen the whole multitude.[8]

As the French advanced in their usual columns the Riflemen skirmishing in front of the British lines began to pick them off from whatever cover they could find while at the same time the gunners, having found their range, mowed down the enemy to cheers from the infantry. Nevertheless, the French merely closed ranks and marched steadily on. Harris

was very soon hotly engaged. Loading and firing away I became enveloped in the smoke I created ... for a few minutes I could see nothing but the red flash of my own piece ... until a friendly breeze clears the space around, a soldier can know no more of his position, what is about to happen, or what has happened – even amongst his own companions – than the dead lying around.[9]

The infantry of General Fane's brigade, to which Harris belonged, waited impatiently for him to give the word to advance. When it came, they responded enthusiastically, driving the French back. Then Harris was almost swept away by the cavalry charge which followed the infantry advance:

I fell while they were charging, and the whole squadron thundered past, just missing me as I lay amongst the dead and wounded. So tired was I, and overweighted with my knapsack and all my shoemaking implements, that for a short time I lay where I had fallen, watching the cavalry as they gained the enemy.[10]

And witnessing a charge carried too far.

Vimeiro was fought on two fronts and the French were worsted twice over. The victory was not followed up, however. Wellesley wanted to advance on Lisbon but was superseded first by Sir Harry Burrard and then by Sir Hew Dalrymple. The result was the Convention of Cintra, which allowed the French to return to France in British ships, taking their loot with them. There was an outcry in

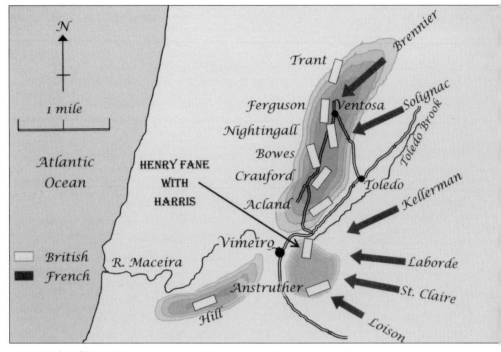

Battle of Vimeiro.

England and the three generals were summoned home to face a court of enquiry. Sir John Moore now took command in Portugal.

After some respite in Lisbon, where he worked in a shoemaker's shop repairing shoes for officers and men alike, Harris found himself once more on the march. Moore advanced into Spain to engage with the Spanish forces which were resisting the French occupation:

> I love to remember the appearance of that army as we moved along. It was a glorious sight to see our colours spread in those fields. The men seemed invincible. Nothing, I thought, could have beaten them … but before a few weeks were over, I witnessed hardship and toil lay hundreds of them low.[11]

The army was in Salamanca when news arrived that the Spanish had been outmanoeuvred and overwhelmed by Napoleon in person. Moore with his 20,000 men was in a perilous situation. Initially, he advanced towards Valladolid to disrupt French communications but the rapid surrender of Madrid necessitated a swift withdrawal. Thus began the retreat to Corunna, at the worst time of the year.

Battle of Vimeiro. (*Author's collection*)

By the time the 95th reached Sahagun on 22 December, the effects of the retreat were becoming clear. Accoutrements, shoes, everything was torn or lost, or had to be destroyed. The situation deteriorated day by day. On 24 December darkness fell on a day without food and only the fierce determination of General Crauford saved many men from collapse and death.

'Black Bob' Crauford was a controversial figure, loved and hated in equal measure. Harris was one of his admirers, respecting the need for the fierce discipline Crauford imposed and recognising his more humane qualities. One night Harris and his front-rank man, Higgins, climbed a steep ascent to get a better view of the French. Crauford found them there:

For many hours the rain had been coming down furiously so, like ourselves, he was drenched to the skin. In his hand he carried a canteen full of rum and a small cup, with which he was endeavouring to refresh some of the men. He offered me a drink as he passed, and then proceeded along the ridge.[12]

It was not only the men who suffered:

Being constantly in the rear of the main body, the scenes of distress and misery I witnessed were dreadful to contemplate, particularly amongst the women and children, who were lagging and falling behind, their husbands and fathers being in the main body of our front.[13]

On 1 January 1809 Crauford took the light brigade to Vigo, while the main force continued to Corunna. The march to Vigo intensified Harris's respect for Crauford:

I never admired any man who wore the British uniform as much as I did General Crauford ... he often addressed me kindly in adverse circumstances when you might have thought that he had scarcely any spirits to cheer up the men under him. The Rifles liked him; but they also feared him; for he could be terrible when insubordination showed itself in the ranks.

But as Harris conceded, 'This was no time to be lax in discipline, and the general knew it for some of the men were becoming careless and ruffianly in their demeanour.'[14]

The light brigade reached Vigo in the middle of January and found transports waiting to carry them back to England. When Harris and his fellow riflemen landed at Spithead they were a sorry sight. 'Many had their clothes and accoutrements in fragments, and some had their heads swathed in old rags. Our weapons were covered with rust. Quite a few men, from toil and fatigue, had become quite blind.'[15] No wonder the people of Portsmouth were horror-struck.

After a period of recovery, Harris was sent on recruiting duties. By July, though, Harris's company, along with others of the 2/95th, formed part of the infamous Walcheren expedition. At South Beveland, Harris observed the effects of the ague which reduced strong men to shaking wrecks. At Flushing sickness was so widespread, with 11,000 men suffering from 'Walcheren fever' that the expedition could advance no further. Harris finally succumbed to the disease on board ship. In England he was put into an eleven-bedded ward:

Here I lay and saw this ward refilled ten times, the former patients all being carried to the grave ... One or two of my old

Peninsular comrades, men I had often seen fighting bravely on the field, I saw die in this hospital in a miserable condition, their bodies swollen up like barrels.[16]

Harris had earned £200 from repairing shoes and used it to buy wine and other nourishing things for himself, as well as to provide treats for his fellow-sufferers.

This bout of Walcheren fever effectively brought Harris's military career to an end. He collapsed on the march to Portsmouth when the 2/95th were returning to the Peninsula. Even after a long period of convalescence at home in Dorset and a further period in hospital at Hythe, he was still unfit. In December 1813 he was sent to Chelsea for discharge. A short period in a veteran battalion was brought to an end by Napoleon's first abdication. He was discharged on 10 July with a pension of 6d a day, which he lost the following spring when he ignored a recall to service. Yet, despite the damage to his health, he lived long enough to claim the General Service medal finally awarded in 1847, with bars for Roliça, Vimeiro and Corunna.

Edward Costello was Irish, born at Montmellick in 1788. Unlike Harris, he was a volunteer rather than a balloted man when he joined the Dublin City Militia aged 16. Three years later he enlisted into the 95th. He missed the first expedition to the Peninsula because he was not then fully proficient in light infantry duties. Consequently, he was spared the horrors of the retreat to Corunna, although he witnessed the condition of the survivors, who were in 'a most deplorable state. Their appearance was squalid and miserable in the extreme ... Their clothing was in tatters and in such an absolute state of filth as to swarm with vermin.'[17] Costello did not have long to wait for his own Iberian experiences, however. In May 1810 the 1/95th marched to Dover. On 18 June the battalion sailed to Portugal with the 1/43rd and 1/52nd, two light infantry battalions.

Sir Arthur Wellesley was in central Spain, acting in conjunction with Spanish forces against French armies under Marshal Victor and King Joseph. General Crauford, in command of this re-formed light brigade, was determined to join Wellesley before a battle was fought. 'The excellent orders our Brigadier issued for maintaining order and discipline, though exceedingly unpopular at first, have since become justly celebrated in the service.' Crauford pushed his troops hard but still 'maintained a popularity among the men who, on every other occasion, found him to be their best friend'.[18] It was principally officers like Jonathan Leach who detested Crauford.

Despite undertaking 'one of the longest marches in the military records of any country, scarcely halting', which became mythologised by William Napier in his history of the Peninsular War as 'over 62 miles and in the hottest season of the year in 26 hours', the light brigade arrived an hour too late for Talavera.

Realising that he could not depend upon the Spanish, Wellesley retreated to Portugal. At Elvas, just over the border, Costello contracted typhus fever and was in hospital from August until January 1810, followed by several weeks spent convalescing. He re-joined his battalion in March, now part of the newly-formed light division and still under Crauford's command. The division was holding a position on the River Agueda at Barba del Puerco on the Spanish-Portuguese border while cantoned in the surrounding villages. Every night a captain's piquet was mounted on high ground overlooking a bridge. On the other side the French posted their own advanced sentries.

On 19 March Costello came under fire for the first time, when 3,000 French under General Ferey attacked the outposts of the 95th. Awoken at midnight by the sound of the sentries' rifles and French drums, Costello was soon

> startled out of my lethargy by the whizzing of the enemies' bullets. My astonishment gave place to perfect recollection, and in less than a minute we were all under arms ... I felt an indescribable thrill, for never before had I been under the fire of a French musket.

At Captain O'Hare's order 'We threw ourselves forward amongst the rocky and broken ground, from whence we kept up a galling fire upon those who had commenced storming our heights.' The situation was perilous and the arrival of Colonel Beckwith and three relieving companies was very welcome:

> For a while the contest was doubtful and bloody, but after about half an hour's hard fighting, the enemy were obliged to retreat precipitately, and under a close and murderous fire from us. This was, I believe, the first and last time the French ever attempted to surprise a rifle picket.[19]

The French were besieging the Spanish border town of Ciudad Rodrigo. When it finally fell, despite a determined Spanish defence, the light division was pulled back. Marshal Masséna, in command of the Army of Portugal, made the fortress of Almeida his next objective and Wellington (as he now was) ordered Crauford to bring his division to safety by crossing the only bridge spanning the precipitously-sided Coã. Crauford ignored the order. On 24 July the French attacked with 4,000 infantry, 1,100 cavalry and six guns.

In a desperate encounter the Anglo-Portuguese were driven back to the bridge, inch by hard-fought inch. Some French Hussars, initially mistaken for King's German Legion cavalry, descended on the 95th 'and our men were trampled down and sabred on every side ... A French dragoon seized me by the collar, while several others aimed at me with their swords as they passed.' Costello was saved when the dragoon's horse was brought down:

> The animal was on the dragoon's leg. Determined to have one brief struggle for liberty, I freed myself from his grasp, dealt him a severe blow on the head with the butt of my rifle, and rushed up to our 52nd. I was in the act of clearing the wall at a jump, when I received a shot under the cap of my right knee and fell.

At first Costello was helped towards the bridge by another rifleman piggyback fashion, but when his rescuer was wounded by a bullet which smashed his arm and then penetrated Costello's thigh, his situation was desperate. He managed to cross the bridge

> from the other side of which Captain Ross's guns were in full roar, covering our retreat. In this crippled state, and faint through loss of blood, I made an appeal to another comrade, who assisted me to ascend a hill on the other side of the river.[20]

Now the French took heavy casualties as they tried to cross the bridge. Marshal Ney, in command, lost 1,000 men against 316 Anglo-Portuguese killed, wounded and missing.

The light division retreated swiftly, taking their wounded with them. Costello hobbled along, using a couple of rifles as crutches. At Pinhel the local magistrate provided bullock carts for the most seriously wounded, including Costello. The small vehicle was crammed with men but was still a relief to its occupants. At Freixadas about forty Guards from the 1st division were ordered to succour the injured men and dress their wounds, which they did generously.

Costello did not rejoin his battalion until October, when they were behind the Lines of Torres Vedras. In mid-November Masséna retired to Santarém to await reinforcements that never arrived. His half-starved troops held out until March 1811. Victims of Wellington's scorched-earth strategy, they retreated to Spain, leaving a trail of destruction behind them. The light division were in the van of the pursuit, and fought several limited but fierce actions before winning glory at Sabugal on 3 April. Outnumbered and unsupported, three times forced to concede ground to a superior French force, they held out and finally 'obliged' the French to retreat.

When Masséna crossed into Spain, he left a French garrison stranded in Almeida. His attempt to relieve them was frustrated at the battle of Fuentes de Oñoro, where the light division played a crucial part in rescuing the stranded 7th division, demonstrating to their own satisfaction that they were the elite of the army.

The remainder of 1811 saw the light division holding positions near Ciudad Rodrigo, which Wellington besieged at the beginning of 1812. When an assault was imminent, Costello volunteered for a storming party and considered it his good fortune to be chosen. 'We shook hands with friendly sincerity and speculated on whether we would outlive the assault. If truth must be told, we also speculated on the chances of plunder in the town.'[21]

Whatever Costello witnessed during the attack on the lesser breach, including the death of colleagues and the fatal wounding of General Crauford, it was as nothing to the vision of Hell that was the assault of Badajoz nearly four months later. This time he was in the ladder party, and did not expect to survive. As the light and 4th divisions drew closer to the breaches in the dark,

> The French sentry challenged. This was instantly followed by a shot from the fort and another from the walls of the town. A moment afterwards a fire-ball was thrown out. It threw a bright red glare of light around us. Instantly a volley of grape-shot, canister and small arms poured in among us as we stood on the glacis about 30 yards from the walls.

Three of the ladder party were killed by this attack, and Costello toppled backwards. 'Our men were falling fast. The remainder of the stormers rushed up, disregarding my cries, and those of the wounded men around me. Many were shot and fell upon me, so

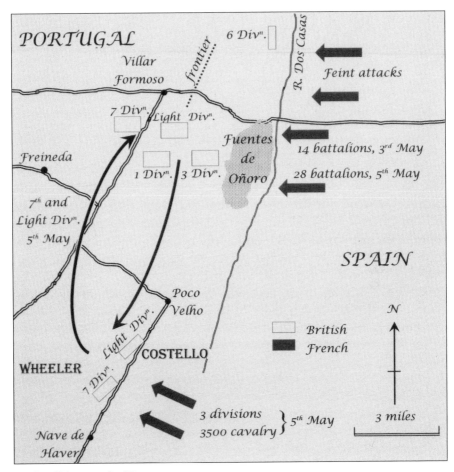

Battle of Fuentes de Oñoro.

that I was drenched in blood.' Finally extricating himself but not his rifle, Costello rushed towards the breach, sword in hand. Again he was knocked off his feet. The French had damned the Rivillas stream:

> To my surprise [I] found myself immersed to my neck in water ... Diving through the water – I was a good swimmer – I gained the other side but in doing so I lost my sword.
>
> I now attempted to get to the breach, which the blaze of musketry from the walls clearly showed me. Without rifle, sword, or any other weapon, I succeeded in clambering up a part of the breach where there was a *chevaux-de-frise*, consisting of a

piece of heavy timber studded with sword blades, turning on an axis. Just before I reached it, I received a stroke to the breast. Whether it was from a grenade, or from a stone, or the butt-end of a musket, I cannot say, but down I rolled senseless, drenched with water and human gore ... While I lay in this position, the fire continued to blaze over me in all its horrors, accompanied by screams, groans, and shouts, the crashing of stones and the falling of timbers. For the first time in many years I uttered something like a prayer.[22]

The town was actually carried by escalade, although the worst carnage was at the breaches, where the light division alone lost 927 officers and men, 193 from the 1/95th. Costello spent another two months in hospital, although not before he had made his way into the town, spared a French soldier whom he had been tempted to shoot out of irritation at the pain he was suffering, and witnessed what he described as scenes of wickedness. This did not stop him accepting twenty-six dollars as his share of some plunder, however.

Battle of Fuentes de Oñoro. (*Author's collection*)

Between Badajoz and the Waterloo campaign Costello (like Wheeler) marched to Madrid and then experienced the misery of the retreat back to Portugal. In 1813 he fought at Vitoria, where he acquired a considerable amount of plunder, and in the battles of the Pyrenees. In April 1814 he was at Toulouse when news arrived of Napoleon's abdication, but this was not the last of Costello's war, or of his wounds. At Quatre Bras he was 'in the act of taking aim at some of our opposing skirmishers, when a ball struck my trigger finger, tearing it off. It also turned the trigger aside. A second shot passed through the mess-tin on my knapsack.'[23]

Despite the damage to his hand, Costello eventually re-joined his battalion in France as part of the army of occupation and enjoyed a dramatic affair with a young French woman. Although he was discharged in 1819, he later volunteered as a mercenary in the Carlist Wars of 1835 where gross mismanagement reminded him of the excellence of the Peninsular Army. Married and with a large family, he ended his life as a yeoman warder of the Tower, dying in 1869 at the age of 81.

During the retreat from Corunna, experienced by Harris and reported by Costello, there occurred one of those events which are the stuff of legends. Somewhere near Astorga the French general, Auguste-Marie-François Colbert launched his cavalry against the rearguard, including the 95th. Colbert, on his grey horse, was a tempting target and, the story goes, General Paget offered money to the man who brought him down. Tom Plunket (or Plunkett) of the Rifles ran forward, 'threw himself on his back on the road (which was covered with snow), placed his foot in the sling of his rifle, and taking deliberate aim, shot General Colbert'.[24] He then took out Colbert's trumpet-major before returning to his own lines to general acclamation.

It was a good tale, and appropriate to a man who was in every sense a *character*, a labourer from Wexford with all the virtues and all the weaknesses of his national stereotype. He was 'a general favourite of both officers and men, besides being the best shot in the regiment'.[25] Captain George Miller was with Plunket in South America (1807) and in Spain, later writing accounts of both campaigns. He recalled how Plunket and another rifleman posted themselves on a roof in Montevideo and held off the attackers for several hours. Less admirably, Plunket then shot a Spanish aide-de-camp who rode up carrying a flag of truce.

71

Costello included several references to Plunket in his memoirs. There was the occasion when Plunket was urging men from the Lincoln Militia to join the 95th:

> ... the better to attract the 'awkwards', and to the amusement of a very large crowd, he commenced a shuffle on the head of one of the very large barrels of beer [which had been placed in the street]. After a few steps the head gave way and soused him up to his neck in the liquid.

Nothing dismayed, he went into the nearest public house and climbed part-way up its chimney before reappearing. Then 'giving himself a Newfoundland shake that, in an instance, opened a wide circle of militiamen,' he announced, '"damn your pipe clay – I'm ready for the grand parade."'[26] One of the selling points of the 95th was its lack of army bull.

Plunket enjoyed creating entertainment. On board ship bound for Portugal the

> officers, who were mostly a jolly set of fellows, had recourse to various expedients to while away the time. An extremely popular one was getting Plunket to dance a hornpipe on the quarter-deck to the music of our band. Tom did so famously, and the beating of his feet in the 'double shuffle' drew the loudest plaudits from our men, and from the crew of the vessel.[27]

There was a darker side to Plunket, however. He was promoted to sergeant but alcohol proved his undoing. He appeared drunk on parade and gave orders for inspection in such a manner that it set the men laughing. When ordered to stop by the pay-sergeant he refused. The altercation then drew the attention of Captain Stewart, who placed him under arrest. 'When sober, Tom was noted for his good humour and humanity, but now, left alone, and under the influence of intoxication, he felt that his treatment had been undignified, and wanted vengeance.'[28] He barricaded himself in the guard room with a loaded rifle, ready to shoot Captain Stewart. Forewarned, the captain wisely kept out of his way.

There followed the inevitable court martial. Plunket was sentenced to 300 lashes and reduced to the ranks:

> Flogging is a disgusting subject of contemplation at all times, but in this instance it seemed doubly so now that a gallant, and until

a few days previous, an honoured and respected man was to suffer. Poor Tom had the commiseration of the whole regiment.

Worse followed, because he was unable to take his punishment. As the flogging proceeded,

> Plunket's sufferings became intense. He bit his lip to stifle the utterance of his pangs, but nature was too strong for suppression. More than once, he gave way to a half-agonized cry that seemed to thrill through the blood in [Costello's] view.

After thirty-five lashes Colonel Beckwith ordered the punishment to stop with the comment: 'You see now, sir, how very easy it is to commit a blackguard's crime, but how difficult it is to take his punishment.'[29]

It is not surprising that a larger-than-life character like Plunket should have become the stuff of legend. But legends grow in the telling. It seems that embellishments were added to the killing of Colbert, either by the men who reported the event or by Costello himself.

William Surtees, Quartermaster with the 95th, was not on the scene but close enough to have heard the story soon afterwards. He wrote that Colbert was killed

> by a pickle of the name Tom Plunket, who, fearless of all danger to himself, got sufficiently nigh to make sure of his mark, and shot him, which, with the fire of the others, caused great havoc in the enemy's ranks, and set them to flying in the rear much faster than they advanced.[30]

Captain Miller, a great admirer of Plunket who requested to have him in his company, was on the scene and his account clarifies how the story evolved. According to Miller, there were two French generals, Colbert and Goulieu, the latter riding a white horse. General Graham, rather than Paget, offered money to the man who would 'shoot the fellow on the white horse'.

'"Please your honour," said Plunket, who had just shot General Colbert, "it won't cost you a tester." He missed him, however, as did many others.' Plunket may not have shot the fellow on the white horse, but he did shoot a white horse, with the imperial eagle on its saddle cloth, which had been caught and mounted by Lieutenant Layton of the 95th. 'He fortunately missed Layton, but shot the horse dead. "The fellow," said Layton to me afterwards, "he shot my horse." I told him he might think himself particularly fortunate in not being shot himself, which was certainly intended.'[31]

Two further points are worth noting before we leave the exaggeration of Plunket's deed to legend. Firstly, there is no record of a General (or Colonel) Goulieu; he must have been a more junior officer, or the trumpet-major referred to by Costello. Secondly, in the French accounts Colbert was hit in the left eye and the force of the shot knocked him off his horse, suggesting close range, as does Surtees' account. In other words, there would have been no need for the unusual position Plunket is said to have adopted, although his marksmanship was still crucial.

The last we hear of Plunket comes in Costello's memoirs. When he was Yeoman of the Tower he was visited by Mrs Plunket, a woman (according to Costello) disfigured by an exploding gun at Waterloo, who told him

> in the most plaintive tone, and with many sobs, of poor Tom's death. She and Plunket usually tramped through different parts of the country, procuring a livelihood by selling needles and tapes. While passing through Colchester, Tom suddenly staggered a few paces, fell down, and expired ... Thus ended the career of the gallant but unfortunate Plunket.[32]

Researching Benjamin Harris, Edward Costello and Tom Plunket

The memoirs of Benjamin Harris and Edward Costello are well-known and easily accessible through several different editions, some with considerable editorial input and others merely a reprint of the original texts. The two men recreate the experiences of the 95th Rifles through vivid recollection of both the dramatic and the more mundane experiences of the men in the ranks. They also provide a significantly different perspective from the journals and memoirs written by officers of the regiment, men like Harry Smith, Jonathan Leach, George Simmonds and John Kincaid, the most entertaining of all. Indeed, the wealth of material produced by officers and men of the 95th explains the dominant position this regiment occupies in the public consciousness, instanced in particular by Bernard Cornwell's *Sharpe* novels and also by the large number of Green Jackets at Napoleonic re-enactments.

It is important to remember, however, that Harris and Costello were recollecting events long past. This is significant for Costello, whose first memoirs appeared in 1839–40, in the *United Services Journal* and were then published in book form in 1841. This means that in their finished form they post-dated all six volumes of William Napier's *History of the War in the Peninsula and the South of France*, as well as some of the memoirs mentioned above, particularly Kincaid's. Costello was literate and may have been influenced by these writers' presentation of events that he had experienced but was now viewing through the mists of time. Harris was illiterate, so that when he was persuaded by Henry Curling, probably in about 1835, to recount his memories he was unlikely to be familiar with any other version of the events he chose to describe. Indeed, in their 1848 form they had the random structure of spontaneous recollection.

With this proviso, Harris and Costello's memoirs can be judged among the most convincing accounts of the Peninsular War, and are invaluable for anyone who wants to understand the viewpoint of these elite riflemen. They vividly convey the thoughts and feelings of the ordinary soldier, their attitudes to war, to their fellow soldiers, and to authority. (It is interesting that they both admired General Crauford.)

Harris and Costello can both be traced through the muster rolls (WO12); in Harris's case those of the 66th and 8th veteran battalion, as well as the 95th. His discharge papers give us the usual encapsulated description; black hair, grey eyes and dark complexion; and confirm his trade as a cordwainer. It is thanks to the researches of Eileen Hathaway that we know the circumstances of his birth and family.[33] She also cites the findings of Jack Stratfull which establish that Harris died in 1858 at the Poland Street Workhouse, Westminster, possibly insane (or more likely suffering from dementia) – a sad end for such a charming memoirist.

Eileen Hathaway has also produced an edition of Costello's memoirs, *Costello: the True Story of a Peninsular War Rifleman*, which not only identifies those points where his memory seems to have deceived him but also fills in the biographical details of his life before and after military service. Furthermore, unlike the other two subjects of this chapter, there exist a portrait and a photograph of the man himself which she reproduces and which brings him closer to the modern reader.

Tom Plunket differs from Harris and Costello in that he wrote no memoirs, leaving us dependent on the recollections of contemporaries like Costello, Kincaid and Miller, as well as modern attempts to establish not only the truth of the legend but also the character of the man himself. George Caldwell, in his book, *Thomas Plunkett of the 95th Rifles: Hero, Villain, Fact or Fiction?*, and Stuart Hathaway, who has posted *Rifleman Thomas Plunkett: a pattern for the Battalion* on www.napoleon-series.org, rigorously explore and analyse all the available evidence. Both come to the conclusion that, whatever the truth of the legend, Plunket was a remarkable man who impressed his fellow soldiers with qualities that went beyond mere expertise as a marksman.

As for researching Plunket, WO12 is again the obvious starting point to outline his career, including promotions and demotions. His discharge papers (WO115 because he was discharged at Kilmainham) tell us that he was born in Newtown, County Wexford, in 1783 and was described as a labourer when he enlisted in 1805. The description of a man 5′ 6″ tall, with brown hair, grey eyes and a pale complexion matches Kincaid's description of a man 'in the prime of manhood; with a clear grey eye and handsome countenance'. Like Harris, he served in more than one regiment; after his twelve years with the Rifles he re-enlisted into the 41st Foot to avoid penury. He also spent three years in various Militia and veteran battalions.

Costello gives a melancholy picture of his final years, but Plunket had chosen to renounce his pension for land in Canada. It was the failure of this enterprise that led to his hard life as a pedlar. He was not forgotten, however, by those who had served with him and when he died in Colchester, in 1851 or 1852 a group of retired officers paid for his funeral and raised money for his widow.

Notes
1. Eileen Hathaway (ed.), *A Dorset Rifleman: The Recollections of Benjamin Harris*, p. 173.
2. Ibid., p. 19.
3. Ibid., p. 36.
4. Ibid., p. 36.
5. Ibid., p. 41.
6. Ibid., p. 42.
7. Ibid., pp. 43–4.
8. Ibid., p. 53.
9. Ibid., p. 55.

10. Ibid., p. 58.
11. Ibid., p. 77.
12. Ibid., p. 95.
13. Ibid., p. 95.
14. Ibid., p. 101.
15. Ibid., p. 106.
16. Ibid., p. 145.
17. Eileen Hathaway (ed.), *Costello, the True Story of a Peninsular Rifleman*, p. 19.
18. Ibid., p. 34.
19. Ibid., pp. 52–3.
20. Ibid., pp. 65–6.
21. Ibid., p. 141.
22. Ibid., pp. 169–71.
23. Ibid., p. 281.
24. Ibid., p. 22.
25. Ibid., p. 21.
26. Ibid., p. 26.
27. Ibid., p. 27.
28. Ibid., p. 41.
29. Ibid., pp. 42–3.
30. William Surtees, *Twenty-Five Years in the Rifle Brigade*, pp. 90–1.
31. George Caldwell, *Thomas Plunkett of the 95th Rifles*, p. 101 (Captain George Miller's account).
32. Costello, p. 315.
33. Harris, p. 15.

Chapter Five

TO THE LAST CARTRIDGE

Wilhelm Wiese and Simon Lehmann of the King's German Legion

As day broke on the morning of 18 June 1815 and men stirred stiffly, cold and damp in the gloom of a grey dawn, not one of the 70,000 men in the Duke of Wellington's allied army could have doubted that they were about to take part in a struggle of titanic proportions. British, German, Dutch and Belgian, they had endured a miserable night after a day when they had retreated in pouring rain from Quatre Bras to this ridge that the Duke had chosen for his stand against the forces of Napoleon Bonaparte, former and restored Emperor of the French. The rain had lashed down in torrents all night, heavier than anything most of them had ever experienced, adding to the despondency attendant upon any retreat.

The old hands, though, the men who had fought with Wellington in the Peninsula, were remembering similar nights, crowned by glorious victories like Salamanca and Sorauren. The auguries were good. Two such men were Simon Lehmann (anglicised to Lehman) and Wilhelm Wiese (anglicised to William), green-jacketed riflemen of the 1st and 2nd light battalions, King's German Legion. Lehmann transferred into the Legion from a Fencible regiment in December 1803. With nine years of service behind him, he was immediately identified as NCO material and promoted to corporal, a position he held for over two years. In April 1805 he was demoted and remained in the ranks for the rest of his time in the Legion. Wiese joined as a recruit five years after Lehmann. Both men served in the Peninsula. The two light battalions joined the Anglo-Portuguese army in 1810 and served with the 1st division until the end of the war. In 1847 Wiese claimed six bars for his General Service Medal. Lehmann could have made the same claim, had he lived to 1847. As it was, his claim to fame was more specific, and made him a hero of the Legion.

On 23 February 1813 the 1st light battalion was one of the units engaged in the crossing of the Adour so that Bayonne could be invested for a siege. There were French gunboats on the river and during the allied shelling the flagstaff of a corvette was shot away. Seeing the ship's ensign as a trophy, Lehmann divested himself of his accoutrements and plunged into the water. Despite being the target of French musketry from the corvette, he swam strongly to the flag and returned with it in triumph. He was rewarded with the proceeds of a whip-round by the officers of the battalion. Being a generous fellow with good taste, he spent the money on bottles of Lafitte which he shared with the men of his company. He was also 'a singular fellow' who had developed a liking for strong liquor during service in the West Indies, but was careful to avoid drinking on duty. Instead, when he received his pay he would seek leave of absence from evening roll call and indulge in a drinking bout for one night only.

In 1814, when the KGL light battalions returned to England from France after Napoleon's first abdication, they must have believed that their fighting days were over. Lehmann actually took his discharge and returned to his family in Hanover. Eleven months later, however, Napoleon escaped from Elba and returned triumphantly to France, whereupon most of the men of the Legion signed up for another six months' service. As a constituent part of the British Army, four of the line battalions and the two light battalions of the Legion, along with cavalry and artillery, were sent to Belgium to form a vital contingent within Wellington's army.

But how did Germans come to be serving in such numbers in the British Army? The answer lies with George III, King of Great Britain and Prince-Elector of Hanover. As far as Napoleon was concerned this made Hanover British territory, to be made an appendage to France. In June 1803 an invading force under General Mortier demanded the total surrender of the Hanoverian army. The Hanoverian government offered neutrality, conceding that its erstwhile soldiers should remain in places designated by the French, and Napoleon was prepared to accept these terms if King George did the same. The King, however, regarded his two territories as distinct from each other, which made the attack on Hanover illegal. Therefore, he refused to ratify the agreement. Napoleon promptly demanded that the Hanoverian army should march to France as prisoners of war, although he later modified this to disbandment and an undertaking that no man would bear arms against France until a similar number of French prisoners had been released from British captivity. On these terms, Hanover and France signed the Convention of the Elbe.

Some of the disbanded army made their way to England, including Lieutenant-Colonel von Decken, who was authorised by the king to raise a force of 4,000 men. Von Decken expected a flood of willing recruits, who were offered similar terms of enlistment and service to British recruits. By the end of August only seven men had enlisted but a month later, by which time the proclamation authorising the formation of the Legion was known in Hanover, several hundred joined, encouraged by their officers.

As volunteers continued to arrive, the King's German Legion was officially incorporated into the British Army[1] and organised into cavalry, infantry and artillery corps, plus a handful of engineer officers.

The infantry comprised eight red-jacketed line battalions and two light battalions which were distinguished by the green jackets otherwise associated with the 5/60th and the 95th Rifles. In 1804 between 4,000 and 5,000 German infantry arrived in the village of Bexhill, Sussex, which remained their base for the rest of the war. Initially, this posting was intended as a defensive measure against the threat of invasion from across the Channel. After Trafalgar and Napoleon's shift of focus to Austria, the Legion became available for foreign service and thus commenced eight years of outstanding military achievement, from Denmark and the Baltic in the north to Sicily and the Mediterranean in the south. But it was the Peninsula which allowed all three arms to demonstrate the qualities which won them the plaudits of their British fellow soldiers.

Of all their actions, two have become iconic: the charge of the 1st and 2nd Dragoons at Garcia Hernandez the day after the battle of Salamanca, when two French infantry squares were broken; and the defence of La Haie Sainte by a single battalion.

The farm of La Haie Sainte was a crucial point in the allied line at Waterloo. Along with Hougoumont to the right and Papelotte to the left, it constituted an obstacle to any French advance towards Brussels. Held by the 2nd light battalion under Major George Baring, the farm

> consisted of a dwelling house, barn, stable, orchard, and garden; one side of the building abutted on the road [from Charleroi to Brussels]; the orchard bounded by a hedge was on that side

looking towards the enemy's position, and the garden, fenced on the road-side by a low wall, and on the other side by a hedge, lay immediately in rear of the whole.

From the courts and buildings two doors and three large gates led to the exterior; two of these entrances were on the road, one opened into the garden, and the others, being the barn and farm-yard gates, were on the west side or allied right of the buildings: of the latter, however, the barn-gate had unfortunately been destroyed previous to the arrival of the German battalion.[2]

The men of the 2nd light battalion, including Wilhelm Wiese, trudged into the farm, wet and weary after the retreat from Quatre Bras, where they had arrived too late to play any significant part in the action. Baring posted his force of 133 officers and 376 NCOs and men; three companies in the orchard, one in the garden, and the remaining two in the buildings. There was no straw to sleep on, but there was meat because Baring ordered the livestock in the farm to be butchered. Foraging also produced peas and wine. Nevertheless, the mood was grim as the hours passed and the rain fell unremittingly.

Behind the farm was the Ohain road, often referred to as the hollow way, where four companies of the 1st light battalion were posted, with two companies further forward, closer to the farm. Among those settling down for an uncomfortable night was Simon Lehmann, hero of the crossing of the Adour. He had re-enlisted on 7 May, just six weeks after his discharge. His motives can only be guessed: the lure of battle, the need to stand with his comrades, or even a sense of unfinished business.

Sleep was well-nigh impossible that night and both battalions roused themselves to a day that promised to be as dismal as the one before. For the defenders of La Haie Sainte there was work to keep them busy. The defences needed to be strengthened; a challenge when the pioneers had been sent to Hougoumont and the battalion possessed no tools, not even a single hatchet. They found the means to make loopholes in the walls, however, and constructed scaffolding to create firing positions, although nothing could be done about the missing barn door. Outside the farm an abattis was built to obstruct the advance of cavalry and a small group of men, including Wiese, was posted to man it.

The sun finally penetrated the greyness. The air warmed and the ground dried. The French were able to drag their guns into position and some time after eleven they roared into life. Their target, however, was not the centre of the allied line but Hougoumont on the right, which was attacked as a diversion to make Wellington reinforce his right wing. When the rest of the line had been weakened the real attack would begin. Unfortunately for Napoleon, Wellington failed to respond to this script, while the commander of the French left, Jérôme Bonaparte, became so determined to take Hougoumont that he waged what was essentially a battle within a battle.

Nearly two hours after the first cannonade, the grand battery on the right of the French line opened up, targeting the allied forces which lay to the left of the Brussels road. Then came the advance of d'Erlon's corp, a swarm of skirmishers as thick as a line of British troops, followed by the columns with their triumphant shouts of 'En avant!' Even as they targeted Picton's division, they milled around La Haie Sainte. The Germans waited – and waited. Only when the right of the French advance was level with the gate of the barn did Baring give the order to fire on the skirmishers.

La Haie Sainte.

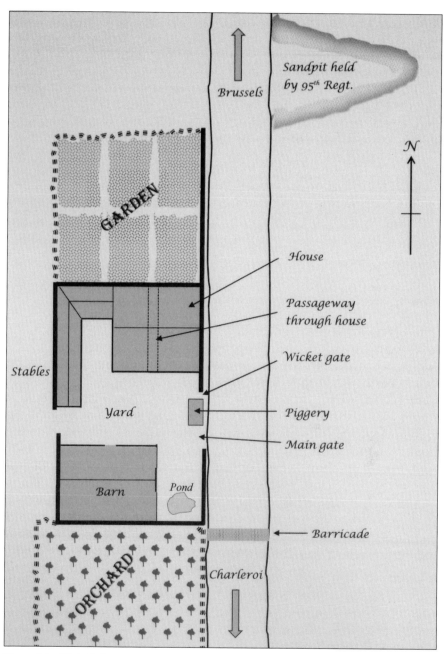

Plan of La Haie Sainte.

The accuracy of the rifles picked off man after man. Even though a lucky French shot broke the bridle of Baring's horse and another killed his second-in-command, Brevet Major Böseweil, this part of the advance was stalled. Indeed, so fierce was the German fire that the French made no attempt to rush the defenders of the barn. Then Lieutenant Graeme opened the wing of the gate to allow a bayonet charge which drove the French back beyond the abattis, manfully defended by Wiese and his companions throughout.

Taking post behind the abattis or frantically strengthening the defences of the buildings, the defenders awaited the next attack, which soon came. The skirmishers were easily dealt with but the advance of the supporting columns forced a withdrawal to the gateway. This was held successfully even though the French threw themselves against the walls and tried to wrest the rifles from the defenders' hands.

Meanwhile, the 1st light battalion had been brought into action in support of Kempt's brigade, on the right of Picton's division, which was engaged in a fierce attack on the head of d'Erlon's left column. Wellington himself gave the order to advance: 'Now is your turn, my lads!' Captain von Gilsa's company was the first to break out of the hollow way, followed by Lieutenant Albert's. This company crossed the Brussels road while von Gilsa's remained on the original side. Both advanced in parallel and fired into the flank of the French troops. This double attack created sufficient confusion to stall the French advance and the bayonet charge which followed sent the French about-turn.

D'Erlon's columns were supported by cavalry, however. In this part of the field, close to the road, Travers' Cuirassiers caused many casualties but just when these armour-plated giants were putting the Germans under critical pressure, more horsemen appeared. Lord Uxbridge (Paget of Corunna fame), in command of the allied cavalry, had sent forward the Household and Union brigades. Closest to the 1st light battalion were the Blues, and they quickly dispersed the cuirassiers and that part of d'Erlon's infantry still threatening La Haie Sainte.

The cuirassiers had, in fact, caused havoc to more than the 1st light battalion. While von Gilsa's company and company number 6, along with the light company of the 5th line battalion and riflemen from three Hanoverian Landwehr units (Verden, Bremen and Lüneburg) were engaged with d'Erlon's infantry, they were protected by the rest of the Hanoverians. Overridden by the cuirassiers, the Hanoverians were thrown into total disarray, causing the garden to be lost. The 2nd light battalion retreated into the farm, including Wiese and his brave colleagues, while the 1st withdrew to the hollow way. At the same time the 5th line battalion, which had been moving forward to support the light troops, was attacked by the triumphant cuirassiers. Still trying to form square and vulnerable to a cavalry charge, they were also saved by the Blues. Less fortunate was the 8th line battalion, which was caught in line and cut down, losing their king's colour. Although the counter-charge of the Household brigade enabled them to rally and re-form behind the hollow way, they were decimated as a fighting force.

Nevertheless, d'Erlon's attack had come to nothing, and La Haie Sainte was still in allied hands.

The next threat was an observed assemblage of French cavalry, cuirassiers, lancers, dragoons and hussars, but when the horsemen moved forward it was obvious their target was the allied centre, not the farm. Nevertheless, the defenders were able to pick off some of the horsemen. And then, from their stronghold, they had the satisfaction of witnessing the cavalrymen's frustration as the allied units formed square and repelled wave after wave of attack.

The situation within La Haie Sainte was increasingly critical, however. Manpower and ammunition were both running low. Reinforcements in the shape of von Gilsa and Marchalck's companies from the 1st light battalion eased the first problem, taking over the defence of the garden. But there was no solution to the low reserves of ammunition, despite Baring's constant messages. Somewhere on the Brussels road was an overturned cart which had been bringing rifle cartridges to the front line. There would be no further supplies. Nor could they raid the pouches of dead Frenchmen because French ammunition, like allied musket balls, was of the wrong calibre. Steadfastness and courage would soon be the defenders' only resources.

The defenders of La Haie Sainte were not the only ones facing a fight against time. After the failure of Marshal Ney's misconceived cavalry attacks, and with the Prussian threat to his right flank growing by the moment, Napoleon realised that if he was to break the allied line he would have to first take the farm. At about five o'clock the defenders once more found themselves under attack as three infantry divisions were sent against them. Another desperate struggle ensued. Once again the accurate fire of the German riflemen held the French at bay. But even the cartridges found in the pouches of their dead and incapacitated comrades provided only a brief respite. Baring, rallying his troops, assured them that fresh supplies would soon arrive. This was a vain hope, although manpower **was** boosted by the arrival of the 5th line battalion and 200 Nassau troops, who immediately displayed the same brave determination as the riflemen.

From the French point of view new tactics were required. The barn was fired. Although there was no straw to create an inferno, smoke and flames were soon rising from the farm. But the intrepid defenders, under Baring's direction, quickly dealt with the threat. They seized the Nassauers' camp kettles and filled them with water from the pond. Some even used their caps for the same purpose. Among these was Wiese who, despite being wounded, continued to play a stout part in the defence of the farm. Even at this critical moment no-one was thinking of surrender. Baring believed that 'So long as our officers fight, and we can stand, we will not stir from this spot.' And so determined was the defence that, against all the odds, the French were once more forced to retire, allowing the Germans further opportunity to strengthen the defences. But time was running out. With only three or four cartridges to a man their firepower would soon fall into silence.

The next French advance was met with yet another fusillade. It was a last act of defiance. The French saw their opportunity and climbed the walls and onto the roofs. Now they could fire down on the defenders. Those who tried to break in through the gates were bayonetted but the fire from above meant a point was quickly reached when resistance was no longer possible. Faced with the reality of annihilation, because the French were not inclined to give quarter, Baring reluctantly gave the order to retire to all but a small force which was left to hold the house. These men were soon overrun and taken prisoner or bayonetted to cries of '*Couyons Hanovriens!*' and '*Couyons Anglais!*'

The survivors of the 1st light battalion and 5th line and the Nassau troops now retired to their units, while Baring brought back to the hollow way just forty-two of the 509 men who started the day as defenders of La Haie Sainte.

And what of Wiese and Lehmann? Wiese survived, despite his wounds, but Lehmann, the volunteer who had come back to finish his fight with the French, lay wounded on the field of Waterloo and

Burying the dead at La Haie Sainte. (*Author's collection*)

would die eighteen days later. He deserved to be remembered, though, because, 'although a simple Hanoverian rifleman, – [he was] worthy of a place amongst the best and bravest of his colleagues'.[3]

Researching Simon Lehmann and Wilhelm Wiese

Because the King's German Legion was incorporated into the British Army and the men enlisted under the same terms as British recruits, the men can be followed through the muster rolls (WO12). These establish, for instance, that Wiese was entitled to the six bars he claimed on his GSM, for Albuera, Salamanca, Vitoria, San Sebastian, Nivelle and Nive. This combination was awarded to all the survivors of the 1st and 2nd light battalions, which arouses some suspicion, but the muster rolls reveal that Wiese was present at all six actions. Similarly, the musters date Lehmann's discharge and rapid return to the ranks. Every battalion that fought at Waterloo had to produce a specific Waterloo muster; that of the 1st light battalion refers to Lehmann's previous service in a Fencible regiment, 1792–1803.

Wiese's arrival in the Legion is more of a mystery. He was recruited on 29 September 1808 and enlisted on 14 October, but the question is, where did he come from? There were several men by the name of Wiese already in the Legion, so that may have been his connection. On the other hand, he could have been recruited as a prisoner of war, since this was one of the most fertile sources of recruits, particularly as many Hanoverians and other Germans had been conscripted to fight for the French. Another possibility is that he had actually escaped to England to join the Legion. Unfortunately, there is no way of selecting from these options.

Men of the KGL were also entitled to pensions, so WO97 is a useful source of biographical detail, although no reference has been found to Wiese in the surviving papers. For officers, WO25 is the repository of their records of service, while PMG6 details officers on half-pay. Other sources of information are the Legion's casualty returns and register of recruits. This register ends in the summer of 1808, too late to record Wiese. A final resource at The National Archives is WO23/135, the Royal Hospital Register of KGL pensions.

Between 1832 and 1837 Ludlow Beamish produced a two-volume *History of the King's German Legion* which drew on the memories of surviving officers. This was reprinted in 1993, and is an invaluable resource which details the history of all the units of the Legion and includes Major Baring's account of the struggle for La Haie Sainte as well as details of the action which led to the award of the Guelphic Medal. Wiese was one of the recipients for his conduct at Waterloo. Had he survived, Lehmann would undoubtedly have been another.

Although Siborne, in his *Waterloo Letters* included only a few of the letters he received from officers of the KGL, Gareth Glover (*The Waterloo Archive Volume II: German Sources*) and John Franklin (*Waterloo: Hanoverian Correspondence*) have made many more available. In addition, the memoirs of Friedrich Lindau of the 2nd light battalion have recently been published in English, while those of Emanuel Biederman, *Von Malta bis Waterloo*, were published in Berne in 1941. Of more general interest are the memoirs of Christian von Ompteda, the most distinguished of the Legion's casualties at Waterloo.

Keeping the best till last, anyone researching an ancestor who served in the KGL can do no better than to contact the Bexhill Hanoverian Study Group. This society, which is dedicated to preserving the memory of the KGL, possesses copious resources including records of births, marriages (usually to local girls) and deaths. As I can testify, they are unstinting in the generous assistance that they give.

Notes

1. There is a tendency for some historians to describe the KGL as mercenaries. If a mercenary is someone who fights for his hereditary ruler in an army which also serves that ruler, then the term is justified but surely this is to stretch the meaning of *mercenary* as it is generally understood.
2. Ludlow Beamish, *History of the King's German Legion*, Volume II, p. 352.
3. Ibid., p. 278.

Chapter Six

BRAINLESS GALLOPERS?

Thomas Jarvis and Andrew Hartley

On 8 November 1808 transports under naval escort arrived in Corunna Harbour with reinforcements for Sir John Moore's campaign in Spain. Aboard these ships were the 7th Hussars, popularly known as 'The Saucy Seventh'. They had been at sea for a month and were now designed as cavalry support for Sir David Baird's infantry contingent, which had already marched to join Moore. The next day half the 745 NCOs and men and 677 horses were landed 'in such a scene of confusion, disorder and mismanagement that we have this day seen [as] was never witnessed'.[1] The horses had to swim a quarter of a mile from the ships to the shore, and then stand for four hours shivering in the cold. Eventually, this part of the regiment was accommodated in a large barn without light, picket posts or breast lines for tethering the horses. To make matters worse, many of the men had found some alcohol and celebrated their arrival on dry land by getting drunk. In the view of the officers, a fine regiment was murdered by this crass mismanagement.

Even though the other half of the regiment was landed more successfully the following day, it was an ominous start to a short campaign that ended disastrously. When the same regiment embarked for England two months later, their effective strength was 150 NCOs and men, and just sixty horses.

The 7th, or Queen's Own Hussars (often still titled dragoons) was a fashionable and wealthy regiment with a fashionable and very able colonel, Henry Paget, later Lord Uxbridge, and a distinguished lieutenant-colonel, Sir Richard Hussey Vivian. The regiment had been changed from dragoons to light dragoons in 1783, and in 1808 had been hussars for a year. Paget was a friend of the Prince Regent and when 'Prinny' designated his light dragoon regiment, the 10th, as hussars Paget requested and gained the same distinction for his own Saucy Seventh. The implications were in the uniform, which, in the

Hungarian fashion, included mustachios (to use the contemporary spelling), furred cloaks and caps.

In their days as light dragoons, the 7th had served under the Duke of York in the Netherlands in 1794, distinguishing themselves at

Hussar uniform. (*Philip Haythornthwaite*)

Beaumont, Willems and Morvaux. Since then, however, they had been on home service.

In 1800 the regiment was recruiting in Lincolnshire and Rutland. In February the recruiting party was in Stamford and one of those they managed to persuade to take the king's shilling was a 19-year-old labourer, Thomas Jarvis, who came from the nearby village of Great Casterton. He was only 5 feet tall, well below the minimum height requirement and unlikely to grow much, but he must have seemed a sufficiently promising fellow because he was allowed to join the ranks.

Eight years later, Thomas Jarvis, briefly a corporal but now reduced to private, was one of those who witnessed the confusion of the landing at Corunna. Worse lay ahead. An officer later wrote: 'I do not suppose there was an army that ever suffered so great hardships and fatigue ... or which suffered greater privations, from want of food and clothing, and rest, exposed night and day to the most inclement weather.'[2]

Within days there were problems. The horses were falling fast and the commissariat was proving itself totally inefficient, so that not only did the men have to shift for themselves but there was no forage for the horses. Every aspect of the march was uncomfortable: dirt, fleas, Spanish antagonism, lack of purpose. But it was even worse for the horses. Galicia was not cavalry country. The horses' feet, made tender by being so long on board ship, were made worse by the rough ground. There was little hay and no oats, only straw and rye, or Indian corn. By the end of November they had lost 150 horses, with the same number of men ineffective.

Leaving men to fend for themselves was also an invitation to misbehaviour, which took the form of repeated drunkenness. And there was also growing resentment, among officers and men, at the lack of direction, as they seemed one day to be advancing and the next day retreating. Even at the beginning of December there was a feeling that 'Ever will the Spaniards rue the day that an Englishman set foot in their country, and never will the British name recover [from] the stigma cast upon it by this cowardly retreat.'[3]

By 4 December, though, the mood had improved as the direction of their march was definitely forwards, taking them towards Salamanca. They passed through Benavente and Toro but then, instead of making for Salamanca, they took the road back to Toro and then on to Tordesillas, which they reached on the 14th. The rain, which had plagued them intermittently since their arrival in Spain, now gave way to extreme cold and frost. It was also about this time news arrived that the French had possession of Madrid. Napoleon, in Spain for the only time, could now deal with Moore. And the French were closer than was generally realised. On 13 December the 18th Light Dragoons encountered a French cavalry force and deprived them of goods worth £30,000 and took twenty prisoners.

At this point there were hopes of a general action but these came to nothing; instead an order arrived for a retreat. As if on cue the misbehaviour increased. Some men were flogged for stealing and drunkenness, in an attempt to stamp out the irregularities. At the same time, the weather continued to deteriorate. Heavy snowfall made the roads very slippery and dangerous for the horses, so the men took to riding through the fields, all the while trying to protect themselves from a piercing north-easterly wind. Indeed, at a later stage of the campaign, a sergeant froze to death in the saddle.

At Sahagun on the 21st there was a sharp encounter between the 15th Hussars, led by Paget, and the French 8th Dragoons and 1st Provisional Chasseurs. A few of the 7th were involved because they were serving as Paget's bodyguard but it is impossible to establish whether Jarvis was among them, even though he received a bar for Sahagun many years later. An officer of the 7th who was a witness, although not a participant, described the action 'as a most scrambling business, being in a Vineyard and knee deep in snow. It however ended in our taking 200 men and horses with little bloodshed.'[4] It was also the first opportunity any of the cavalry had had to test their mettle in a regular engagement with French cavalry since British troops had arrived in the Peninsula.

The ground was now becoming so treacherous that the horses could scarcely stand, and many men took heavy falls. They passed a wet, tiring and definitely un-merry Christmas Day, having had to turn out at five o'clock, hold their position until one o'clock and then ride on to Grajal de Campos, which they reached at six o'clock. Such was the unpleasant business of covering a retreat: 'constant harassment, a great deal of fighting, and very little credit.'[5]

They now learnt that Marshal Soult was nearby with 16,000 men. (Moore's strength was about 13,000 at this stage of the retreat.) By the 28th the British were at Benavente, and the next day the 7th took part in an action with the 10th and 18th Light Dragoons and the hussars of the King's German Legion. The French were seen at the

Trooper, 15th Hussars. (*Philip Haythornthwaite*)

river, which was 2 miles from the town, with a flat plain in between. Although the bridge had been blown up and the river was in spate, the French still managed to get across, whereupon they formed up and attacked the British piquets, including the 7th. There followed a short, sharp action in which the French commander, General Lefebvre-Desnouettes, was taken prisoner under Napoleon's nose. Captain Hodge of the 7th thought Napoleon would never forgive him for the defeat because the French regiments involved, four squadrons of Chasseurs of the Guard, had never been beaten before. Captain Verner believed that Lefebvre-Desnouettes was taken by a man of the 7th, although the King's German Legion maintained that the original captor was a German hussar who was then persuaded by another two men to give up his prisoner.

This was a positive interlude in an otherwise depressing period:

> The men rode the horses as long as they could carry them, they then got off and with the flat of their swords beat them along, and when unable to go further they took off their kit and their cloaks and shot them.[6]

Cruelly and ironically, the lack of nails for horseshoes which caused most of this loss could have been avoided if the stores at Corunna had been brought to the troops.

After passing through Bembibre, where the wine vats were broached with disastrous consequences, the route took Moore's army through the mountains, where cavalry was of little use. Their position at the rear was taken by the infantry. Misbehaviour continued. On 4 January a man of the 7th was shot for plundering. They were marching day and night, many of them on foot:

> ... the road [was] covered with baggage of all sorts, Artillery, men, women and children laying [sic] frozen and freezing to death without a possibility of rendering them assistance, and our horses, with those of the Artillery, so fatigued that they were dropping every hundred yards, where we were obliged to cut their throats and leave them. It snowed the whole way over the mountains and so piercing a wind I never remember.[7]

For the cavalry the end of the campaign was close, unlike the infantry, who still had a battle to fight. By 11 January they were in Corunna. The sick and wounded had been sent ahead and were already on the transports. Further transports were awaited, and for a while it seemed there was to be no escape. Eventually, more ships arrived from Vigo but before they could be boarded there was a last melancholy duty to perform. Only sixty horses could be brought back to England. The rest were shot.

Jarvis embarked on the transport *Sykes*, a fortuitous decision. Those who were on the *Despatch* were lost off Cornwall; three officers, between sixty and seventy men and thirty horses. There were only six survivors, who reported that the captain had been drunk.

On 2 February, within days of landing in England, Jarvis was promoted to corporal for the second time, testimony to his good behaviour during the campaign. There would be no further demotions.

Four and a half years later Jarvis and the 7th Hussars were back in the Peninsula. Some active recruiting, in which Jarvis had played a part in Ireland for two six-month periods, had brought the regiment up to strength. In 1812 they had been at Windsor on royal duty, deputising for the Household brigade which had been sent to the Peninsula. The 7th followed them in the summer of 1813, although too late for the battle of Vitoria.

There had been further promotion for Jarvis during the period of home service. In August 1812 he was made sergeant. From the time the regiment arrived in the Peninsula until its departure a year later he was returned as orderly. This meant he was in attendance on a general or other senior officer, and was a prestigious appointment because only the best-behaved NCOs would be considered for this particular service. The 7th were in Somerset's brigade, but Brigadier-General Vivian, still lieutenant-colonel of the 7th, was in command of another hussar brigade and there is later evidence to suggest that Jarvis was his orderly. Vivian would certainly have known him well.

By the time the 7th joined Wellington's army, the action had moved to the Pyrenees, which gave little scope for the cavalry apart from some piquet and intelligence work. It was also a dangerous place for cavalry:

> … our march was by the Pass of Roncesvalles which is little better than a pass for mules; we were obliged to go by single Files … and even so sometimes with difficulty and not without great danger. Had one of the horses made a false step and gone over, the probability is he would have fallen down an immense precipice into the river. One of our men had a miraculous escape.

His horse fell over and in the fall the man caught hold of a tree and saved himself, but the horse must have been killed.[8]

By the spring of 1814, when the army was in France, the cavalry rejoined. The first action in which the 7th played an active part was at Orthes on 27 February when they distinguished themselves, in

THE OLD SAUCY

SEVENTH,

Or Queen's Own Regt. of

Lt. Dragoons.

COMMANDED BY THAT GALLANT AND WELL KNOWN HERO,

Lieut. General

HENRY LORD PAGET.

YOUNG Fellows whose hearts beat high to tread the paths of Glory, could not have a better opportunity than now offers. Come forward then, and Enrol yourselves in a Regiment that stands unrivalled, and where the kind treatment, the Men ever experienced is well known throughout the whole Kingdom.

Each Young Hero on being approved, will receive the largest Bounty allowed by Government.

A few smart Young Lads, will be taken at Sixteen Years of Age, 5 Feet 2 Inches, but they must be active, and well limbed. Apply to SERJEANT HOOPER, at

─────

N. B. This Regiment is mounted on Blood Horses, and being lately returned from SPAIN, and the Horses Young, the Men will not be allowed to HUNT during the next Season, more than once a week.

─────

BOOTH AND WRIGHT, PRINTERS, NORWICH.

Recruitment poster for the 7th Hussars. (*National Army Museum*)

ground that was unsuitable for cavalry because of its broken nature, by pursuing the defeated French and taking 600 men as prisoners. The 7th themselves thought they had taken anything between 700 and 1,000, as well as just missing an eagle. Whatever the truth of that, they received Wellington's commendation: 'The 7th Hussars distinguished themselves upon this occasion and made many prisoners.' This was rare praise because Wellington was more inclined to criticise his cavalry for their tendency to gallop out of control.

In 1848 Jarvis received four bars on his General Service Medal, for Sahagun and Benavente in 1808 and Orthes and Toulouse in 1814. He may not actually have taken part in the 7th's pursuit of the French if he was orderly to Vivian, but in that case he would certainly have been involved at Croix d'Orade on 8 March, part of the extended action at Toulouse. On this occasion Vivian, with the 18th Hussars, drove the French piquets out of the village of St Loup, then charged the bridge at Croix d'Orade where he routed the 5th and 22nd Chasseurs. Vivian rode with the hussars and took a serious wound. Jarvis was luckier and came through unharmed, even though as orderly he would have been close to Vivian.

After Napoleon's first abdication the 7th might have expected to return to a peaceful country on the other side of the Channel. Instead they found England convulsed by agitation about the Corn Laws, which raised the price of wheat during periods of shortage to protect the interests of landowners but left the poorest to starve. The army was used to keep the peace and the 7th were brought from Brighton, where they had initially been posted, to West London. Instead of dealing with riots, however, they found themselves anticipating another encounter with the French. When news of Napoleon's return from Elba reached England, they were sent back to Brighton and then received orders for Flanders.

During this short interlude in England Jarvis had received further promotion, to troop sergeant-major, a non-commissioned rank for which there was no infantry equivalent at this time.

When the 7th arrived in Belgium they were stationed near Grammont. Here they were reunited with their Colonel, Henry Paget, now Lord Uxbridge, who was returning to active service for the first time since Corunna. He drilled them three times a week. Jarvis, however, was appointed orderly to Major-General Vivian as soon as he arrived in Belgium. Because he was now on the general list, Vivian was no longer lieutenant-colonel of the 7th, but he obviously looked to his old regiment for an orderly he could depend upon.

On 16 June Vivian's 6th brigade was hurried to Quatre Bras but arrived too late to be part of the action. The following morning it was posted on the left of Wellington's position as he waited for the French, who had been worsted but not comprehensively defeated the previous day, to make a move. Eventually Wellington began to pull his army back, leaving his cavalry to mask this manoeuvre. When the French finally reacted, the cavalry withdrew according to orders that had already been issued. Vivian's brigade, along with Vandeleur's 4th brigade, retreated along cobbled lanes east of Genappe. By the time they reached the village of Thy, where there was a bridge across the Dyle, the French cavalry was in close pursuit. Vandeleur, in front, took up a position on a plateau of higher ground while Vivian's brigade engaged in increasingly fierce skirmishing with the enemy. Vivian anticipated that Vandeleur would hold his ground as the 6th brigade retired, and would then take up the fight so that the 6th brigade could reform, classic cavalry tactics. Instead, Vandeleur withdrew to the bridge.

The three hussar regiments that made up Vivian's brigade, the 10th, 18th and 1st KGL Hussars, were now hard-pressed. Vivian sent an urgent message to Vandeleur to get across the bridge as quickly as possible. At this point, to add to their woes, the heavens opened. Vivian held his position for as long as possible, to give Vandeleur time to get his units across the bridge and then sent the 10th and the 18th to join them. This left the German hussars in a perilous position, until they discovered a sunken lane and a second bridge. The French shifted their attention to the main bridge, but their attempts to cross it were frustrated by the fire of the 10th, who were lined up on the opposite bank. With the enemy driven off, the two brigades could continue their route to Waterloo.

This was an unpleasant experience for Jarvis, but his comrades in the 7th suffered an even worse fate when they were halted at Genappe, and were promptly set upon and overrun by French lancers. They suffered heavy casualties, including Major Edward Hodge who was killed, before they were rescued by the Life Guards. Captain Verner later recorded that his squadron was reduced by nearly one half.

Like the rest of the allied army, Vivian's brigade arrived at Waterloo wet, cold and hungry. After a miserable night when sleep

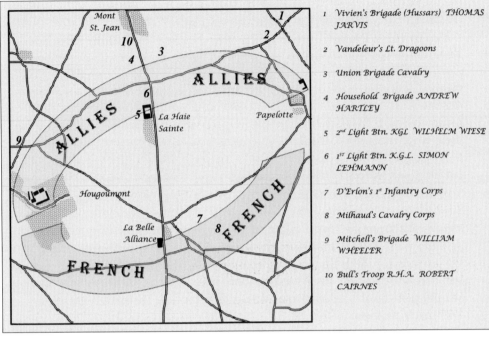

1 Vivien's Brigade (Hussars) *THOMAS JARVIS*

2 Vandeleur's Lt. Dragoons

3 Union Brigade Cavalry

4 Household Brigade *ANDREW HARTLEY*

5 2nd Light Btn. KGL *WILHELM WIESE*

6 1st Light Btn. K.G.L. *SIMON LEHMANN*

7 D'Erlon's 1st Infantry Corps

8 Milhaud's Cavalry Corps

9 Mitchell's Brigade *WILLIAM WHEELER*

10 Bull's Troop R.H.A. *ROBERT CAIRNES*

Battle of Waterloo.

The 7th Hussars and Life Guards at Genappe. (*M.K.H. Crumplin*)

was difficult, they faced the next day tired and jaded. They were posted on the extreme left of the allied position, north of Papelotte, and patrolled as far south as Smohain, where it was hoped the Prussians would make their appearance. They were spectators when the two heavy brigades, the Union on the left and the Household on the right, made their great charge against d'Erlon's corps, which was threatening to break the allied line. They remained helpless spectators as the exhausted Union brigade was overwhelmed by cuirassiers and lancers. Neither Vivian nor Vandeleur dared to come to their help without specific instructions from Wellington. Vandeleur finally cracked and brought his light dragoons, supported by some Dutch light cavalry, to the aid of the heavies, taking considerable casualties. Vivian also eventually offered some support, although rather more cautiously.

It was not until the fall of La Haie Sainte that Vivian's brigade became fully engaged. By this point the Prussians were arriving from the east, so that the two light cavalry brigades could be brought west of the Brussels to Charleroi road without the risk of the French turning the allied left. And they were needed, to support the beleaguered allied infantry in the centre. It would seem, moreover, that Vivian acted on his own initiative this time, and was already at the main road when he met Uxbridge bringing orders for him to perform the very manoeuvre he was actually performing. Not only did the arrival of the two brigades give confidence to the infantry, but they themselves saw off French cavalry at every opportunity.

Once the French were in retreat, Vivian led the 10th against some enemy cavalry attempting to make a stand. Having dispersed these horsemen, he then rode back towards the 18th. At this point he was attacked by a cuirassier. Vivian had lost the use of his right arm at Toulouse and all he could do with it was hold the reins, so he thrust at his assailant with his sword in his left hand and wounded him in the neck. Then 'his little German orderly' cut the cuirassier down. Jarvis was not German but he was certainly small. Vivian wrote his account of what happened in 1841, a year before he died, when his memory seems to have been failing. It is just possible that the little orderly was Jarvis, who certainly would have been in close vicinity.

Whereas Thomas Jarvis's memories of Waterloo were likely to have been of the later stages of the battle, another cavalryman on the battlefield, Andrew Hartley of the Royal Horse Guards, or Blues, would probably have remained haunted by much earlier events.

Hartley, a Yorkshireman from Lofthouse, had been recruited into the Blues aged 18 in March 1809 and when he joined the regiment it was serving at Windsor. As a royal regiment its most important duty, from its establishment in 1661, was to guard the sovereign. Indeed, there was only one extended period, from 1763 to 1804, when this duty was not performed. In 1793 the Horse Guards accompanied the Duke of York to the Netherlands and, like the 7th, conducted themselves well. This was their only active service since 1763. The regiment remained at Windsor until 1812, when they were sent to Lancashire to prevent the machine-breaking activities of some Luddites. Later the same year they were warned for foreign service, and on 10 October two squadrons embarked at Portsmouth.

Trooper, Royal Regiment of Horse Guards. (*Author's collection*)

This same day Hartley began a journal which he kept throughout his time in the Peninsula. He started by noting that the twenty-one officers, twenty-four NCOs, four trumpeters, 290 rank and file and 264 horses were dispersed among eight transports where, had he known it, they were to spend rather longer than they might have wished. There followed violent storms and inevitable seasickness, 'so that there was not a soldier on board but was affected in a lesser or greater degree', and the ships remained off the Isle of Wight. On the 22nd, which was Hartley's 22nd birthday, he was made corporal. The storms also blew themselves out this day. Four days later the transports with the Life Guards, the other regiment of the Household brigade, joined them, whereupon 'we alternately cheered each other as they passed us, which has the most animating effect'.[9] Finally, on 8 November, they got under sail with a favourable north-easterly wind.

Hartley's sentiments at this point are probably typical of the time:

The night coming on we soon lost sight of the chalky cliffs of Albion which perhaps fate has decreed I shall never see more. Tho' I was pleased that we had got under sail yet a sort of melancholy pervaded my feelings. Dear native land adieu, may nothing but peace & happiness come within thy borders, may those rocky bulwarks that are almost lost to the night accompanied with thy naval powers still secure thee from the merciless fangs of haughty Gaul and may commerce flourish with all its attendant blessings which together with thy native courage has made thee what thou art. The envy & dread of thine enemies and the wonder & admiration of thy friends & surrounding nations.[10]

On 21 November the fleet of transports, with its naval escort, finally sighted land. By eleven o'clock that night they were at anchor in Lisbon harbour and the following afternoon they disembarked and marched to Belem. Here they remained until the end of November, when they went 4 miles up-country into the hills and their new quarters in the village of Luz. This place 'had a very romantic appearance, large hills hiding their heads almost in the clouds, having pleasant cottages at their feet with gardens, pleasure grounds and vineyards scattered about in the most beautiful profusion'.[11] From here Hartley went nearly every day to Lisbon for orders as the regiment's orderly corporal. He admired the 'public edifices' and 'noble statues' of the Portuguese capital, but deplored the dirt in the streets. Nevertheless, the place fascinated him and he devoted several pages of his journal to an extended description of the city, its inhabitants and their lifestyle.

The war could not be forgotten, however, and he recorded on 3 December that 'Lord Wellington has been obliged to retreat a very considerable way with the French harassing his rear, his head quarters are now at Freinada.'[12] He also heard from Major Hill of the regiment, who had experienced both, that this retreat from Burgos was worse than Corunna.

There were inspections to pass the time, by Field Marshal Beresford and Lieutenant-General Sir Stapleton Cotton, the latter in command of the cavalry, when the regiment was fulsomely complimented for its fine military appearance and the good condition of the horses. But there were two dangers when a regiment was inactive: sickness (exacerbated by the rainy season) and misbehaviour. 'There are many of our men sick of fluxes and fevers,' Hartley wrote on 20 December. 'I am very bad myself & am afraid I shall be obliged to give up my duty for the present.'[13] In fact, he finished up in the regimental hospital, although he was fit to march on 11 January when they finally left Luz.

As for misbehaviour, some of the more unprincipled men, as Hartley labelled them, had behaved so badly that the locals retaliated by stabbing them, in two cases fatally. Hartley himself had no doubt where to place the blame.

Their new headquarters were at Tomar, 84 miles from Luz and closer to the cantonments of the army. They arrived on 17 January, and almost immediately learnt that Wellington had become their colonel, and had appointed them to serve with the Life Guards under Major-General Robert Hill, attached to the 1st division. This was all good news, but it could not disguise a very real problem for the cavalry (and for the artillery), shortage of forage which effectively prevented any advance against the French. In fact, it kept the whole army immobile because infantry needed cavalry and artillery support. Still, Tomar was a pleasant town, rations were good, wine was cheap, and the people quickly grew fond of the regiment, so that there was general regret when they finally departed on 19 April for Castello Branco.

They now spent most of the next five weeks on the march, finally reaching Salamanca on 28 May. Although Hartley did not seem to realise it, since his journal merely records where they were day by day, the 1813 campaign was now under way. At Salamanca they encountered the light division. Costello remembered how

> We beheld them drawn up at the side of the road and their fresh, well-fed appearance gave rise to many jests at the 'householders' expense. I learnt that because of our dark clothing and embrowned visages, they took us for a foreign regiment.[14]

Hartley made no comment on the 95th, but he did take the opportunity to explore Salamanca, the magnificence of which almost overwhelmed him, and went to the theatre to see an 'insipid comedy'.

From Salamanca their route took them to Vitoria where, on 21 June, they had every hope of going into action; but

> We did not come into action tile [sic] about 3 o'clock P.M. when our brigade formed a close column with 4 others about a league from Vitoria & we expected & ardently wished to have an opportunity of charging their retreating columns but this was denied us, their retreat was so rapid we could not come up with them. We passed Vitoria a little to the left about ½ past 4 o'clock and the French having gained a chain of mountains about a league to the S.E. of Vitoria made another stand and formed line. Our brigade was ordered to cover the 4th division and a brigade of artillery, the ground being so intersected with ditches were [sic] it was level and a continual succession of hills that it was impossible to charge them. They however did not stop tile [sic] we could come near them for having seen the right wing of our army marching with rapidity in another direction to surround them, which would have been accomplished in a short time had they stood, they moved off with great precipitation, leaving their baggage, ammunition and every thing except themselves to our mercy.[15]

Hartley then recorded in detail the riches that were available to the pursuing troops but implied that plundering was limited to flour, bacon and other comestibles. The next day, though, he was less ingenuous:

> 133 cannon were taken yesterday, great quantities of baggage and plenty of their cattle are about the roads – we have likewise taken their military chest in Vitoria said to contain 3 million

dollars, many hundreds of individuals likewise (particularly amongst the infantry and those with the baggage) have enriched themselves.[16]

The campaign now took them towards the Pyrenees, terrain even less suitable for heavy cavalry than light cavalry, who could still do some outpost work. Consequently, Hartley could only report and comment on the deeds of others, which led him to reflect on the realities of war as he looked on the fires of both armies:

> ... thousands of those armies shall pay the greatest tribute Tyrants can enforce, their lives. And others, still more unfortunate, live on to drag a wretched existence carrying with them to the grave the bullet or the sabre's gash and eat the bitter bread of misery while their country gives with reluctant hand the scanty ill grudged pittance.[17]

At the end of the summer most of the cavalry was quartered in villages around Logroño where Hartley had time to observe the strange method of harvesting practised by the local inhabitants, displaying knowledge that suggests his own background was agricultural. Here they passed the winter and first ten weeks of 1814. In the middle of March they advanced towards France via the towns of Vitoria and Tolosa. At Oruña, a village near the sea, they were joined by a further six officers, 157 men and 151 horses, bringing their strength to 496 men and 449 horses. By 25 March they were in France, riding over 'intolerably bad' roads in incessant rain. But once again, Hartley was giving much of his attention to the local agriculture. He was particularly struck by how

> The fair sex appear to have large portions of labour allotted to them, it is their task to prepare the flax, spin it and make it into cloth which a great many of the peasantry or farmers do all in their own houses. I have likewise seen them holding the plough and assisting in tilling the ground.[18]

Such observations remind us that many soldiers had much more to think about than fighting, or even more general military matters.

Hartley was both impressed and relieved by the way operations in France were proceeding:

> This is certainly a wonderful method of conquering a country. We march, receive our billets and rations as regular as in

England and are received by the inhabitants at the end of the day's march with far greater kindness (if fear does not intervene) than we should be in our native land and as we are in the rear of the army that have generally passed this way, this argues that our forerunners have conducted themselves honorably [sic].

He definitely approved of the strict discipline, imposed by provost marshals, staff corps and military police, and reinforced by Wellington's general orders. 'This strict discipline is certainly the most essential as well as honorable means of carrying on warlike operations in an enemy's country.'[19]

In 1847 Hartley claimed two bars, for Vitoria and Toulouse, although at the latter the cavalry merely conducted a covering operation. Within days news arrived of Napoleon's abdication, or as Hartley expressed it, 'the olive branch of peace is held out to the suffering nations of Europe …Buonaparte [sic] has resigned his usurped crown',[20] and the British soldiers could think of home. The cavalry was to march to Calais, with the Horse and Life Guards bringing up the rear. They set off on 30 May and finally reached Boulogne, which turned out to be their embarkation point, on 14 July. Ten days later they sailed for England, whereupon Hartley ended his journal on a disturbing note:

> I now once more tread on British ground, but without that hilarity, or extravagance of joy which some people pretend to feel on similar occasions; experience has taught me that any country is better for a British soldier than his own; and before night I heartily wished myself at a distance from the shores of Albion.[21]

The returning veterans, after their short, quiet war, were reunited with the men at the depot and resumed their duties at Windsor. Nine months after leaving the Continent, however, they were in Belgium, arriving at Ostend on 4 May. The troop to which Hartley belonged was not with them, although for reasons which are not clear Hartley had been detached and accompanied the squadrons that would serve at Waterloo.

The Blues were quartered at Leiderkerke and other villages near Ninove, which was the cavalry headquarters. With the two regiments of the Life Guards and the 1st Dragoon Guards they again formed the Household brigade, under Major-General Lord Edward Somerset.

For the next five weeks they were occupied with field days and reviews but on 16 June they were ordered to march by way of Braine-le-Comte and Nivelles to Quatre Bras. Like the 7th, they arrived too late for the battle, and spent the night bivouacking in a field between Quatre Bras and Genappe. The next day they retreated. At the point where the Life Guards rode to the rescue of the 7th, they acted as a covering force. Then they rode on to Waterloo, to share the misery of a bivouac and a wet night.

The heavy brigades, both the Household and the Union, played a crucial part in the early stages of the battle on the 18th:

> ... the brigade of Lord Edward Somerset was formed across and extended to the right and left of the high road leading from Brussels to Charleroy [sic], which intersected the British [i.e. Anglo-allied] position nearly in the centre. Gradually advancing from this station, it made several charges, in all of which the French were repulsed. One of these charges was particularly remarkable for the brilliant success with which it was attended. In the hope of penetrating the British position, the attacks of the enemy's powerful cavalry were constantly directed against the centre; it was thus that the cuirassiers and lancers of the Imperial Guard were brought into contact with the Royal Regiment of Horse Guards, near the farm of La Haie Sainte; and it was there that those boasted victors of an hundred fights were in an instant routed and rolled to the earth 'in most admired disorder', by the impetuous charge of the British Household Brigade.[22]

The Household brigade had charged with the Union brigade against d'Erlon's corps. Significantly, the Blues had been held back as a reserve and were in a position to rescue the rest of the brigade when it came under French counter-attack, unlike the Scots Greys, who should have performed the same function for the Union brigade but were carried away by the excitement of the charge. Only 200 strong, the Blues took 50 per cent casualties, but their intervention was crucial in enabling a skeleton heavy brigade to survive and play its part against the later great French cavalry charges.

The name of Andrew Hartley is not in the Waterloo Medal Roll, but the Waterloo muster in the regimental records makes clear that he was a Waterloo Man. On 13 July he received his reward for good service when he was promoted to corporal-major. More would follow and Hartley died many years later still a military man.

The Household Brigade advances at Waterloo. (*M.K.H. Crumplin*)

Researching Thomas Jarvis and Andrew Hartley

When Thomas Jarvis was discharged in 1818, the reason given was redaction of the regiment. After Napoleon's defeat at Waterloo, most two-battalion regiments lost their second battalion, while single-battalion regiments saw a reduction in numbers. Jarvis's discharge papers, however, also contain the information that he was suffering from rheumatism, a condition which could be ascribed to his service in the Peninsula. As a result he received a pension of a shilling a day. The papers also outline his periods at different NCO ranks: four years forty-five days as corporal, although this totals two periods at this rank; four years ninety-seven days as sergeant; and three years 341 days as troop sergeant-major. There is also the comment that his 'general conduct as a soldier' has been good, and 'is hereby recommended from length of services'. There is also the usual biographical description; in Jarvis's case that he had brown hair, hazel eyes and a fresh complexion. As for the biographical details, he is returned as a labourer upon enlistment, which is definitely a catch-all term at this time. Particularly for men from a rural background, it may cover a specific rural skill. For example, a sergeant killed at Waterloo was described as a labourer in one casualty return and as a thatcher in another. In the case of Thomas Jarvis, the term 'labourer' provokes the question, was he literate before he entered the army or was literacy a skill he acquired in the army? He would certainly have needed to be literate by the time he was promoted to sergeant.

Andrew Hartley is not to be found in WO97 for the simple reason that his promotion to corporal-major was not the high point of his military career. In 1822 he was commissioned as quartermaster in the Blues.

Unlike Jarvis, there can be no doubt that Hartley was literate when he came into the army and his unpublished journal is the work of a thoughtful and observant young man possessed of a wide vocabulary and extensive general knowledge. The letters, journals or memoirs of such men always raise questions about their motives in joining the army. Wheeler, for example, similarly thoughtful and well-read, was balloted into the army. Hartley, however, was a willing volunteer. Yet within a few years he had developed a cynical awareness of how little the people of Britain cared for their soldiers.

He also made the significant progression from NCO to officer, not as rare as is sometimes assumed, but definitely a progression only achieved by the outstanding minority. Indeed, for a man even to become an NCO was an indication of exceptional abilities.

When Jarvis was discharged in 1818 he returned to civilian life in the part of the country where he had been born. The census returns of 1841 and 1851 reveal that he was married and had settled in the village of Great Gonerby, just outside Grantham. Combined with his certificate for his second or possibly his third marriage, the census returns tell us that he worked as a baker and shopkeeper. This was a lucrative occupation on the Great North Road in a village at the top of a steep gradient, where mail coach passengers had to walk the last mile. After the death of his wife in 1852, he moved to Baston, a village near Spalding, where he died in 1853.

Hartley, in contrast, continued his military career beyond his association with the Blues. He resigned his commission on 1 January 1831, but he remained on half-pay until his death thirty years later. On 20 December 1830, however, he had been commissioned as lieutenant in the East Kent Yeomanry and served as adjutant from the beginning of 1831. In 1837 there was an accident with a cannon which cost him his hand. When William IV heard what had happened he made Hartley a military (or poor) knight of Windsor. These were retired army officers who received a pension and accommodation at Windsor Castle in return for officiating on occasions like Garter ceremonies. Hartley continued his association with the East Kent Yeomanry beyond this date, being promoted to captain in 1841, and in 1851 was still living near Ashford where he had settled with his

Andrew Hartley.
(*Philip Haythornthwaite*)

wife and son after he resigned his regular commission. He died in February 1861 at Windsor.

Hartley is also a good example of the need to look for variant spellings. In the musters of the Horse Guards his surname is consistently spelled as Hartley. There is no Andrew Hartley in the Army Lists, however, because he himself spelled it as Heartley, the spelling which is also found on the census returns.

Notes
1. The unpublished journal of Captain Edward Hodge.
2. *The Reminiscences of Captain William Verner*, p. 13.
3. Hodge.
4. Ibid.
5. Ibid.
6. Verner, p. 16.

7. Hodge.
8. Verner, p. 25.
9. The unpublished journal of Andrew Hartley.
10. Ibid.
11. Ibid.
12. Ibid.
13. Ibid.
14. *Costello: The True Story of a Peninsular Rifleman*, p. 212.
15. Hartley.
16. Ibid.
17. Ibid.
18. Ibid.
19. Ibid.
20. Ibid.
21. Ibid.
22. Packe, *An Historical Record of the Royal Regiment of Horse Guards*, pp. 118–19.

Chapter Seven

WITH THE GUNS
Benjamin Miller and Robert Cairnes of the Royal Artillery

T he artillery arm of every Napoleonic army was a force apart. The men were both soldiers and technicians, and their presence on the battlefield could make the difference between victory and defeat. Napoleon, who made his reputation in 1793 as a gunner at the siege of Toulon, observed: 'Great battles are won by artillery.' An exaggeration, but as he further noted: 'A good infantry is without doubt the backbone of the army, but if it had to fight long against superior artillery it would be discouraged and disorganized.' Furthermore, there is little doubt that far more battlefield casualties were caused by the guns rather than by muskets, swords or sabres.

In Britain, the distinction between artillery and the other two arms was even more marked because the blue-jacketed artillerymen were controlled not by Horse Guards but by the Master General of the Ordnance. The highly-trained officers, not surprisingly, saw themselves as a race apart, a view shared by the men in the ranks. In his diary, which later became the basis of his journal, Benjamin Miller rarely referred to the activities of other units while Robert Cairnes' letters to his stepfather, also a gunner, focus almost entirely on Royal Artillery matters.

Miller was a Dorset man who enlisted into the artillery in 1796 aged 20 because he could not live on the money he made as an apprentice glove-maker. From the start the life suited him: 'Went to drill, liked it very well, being well used.'[1] In this first flush of enthusiasm he volunteered for service in Gibraltar only a month after he arrived at Woolwich for training.

His initial impression of Gibraltar was probably shared by many other British soldiers who found themselves in alien lands. It seemed an enchanted land. He was fascinated by the wagon-loads of oranges

113

and the diversity of the inhabitants, who seemed to come from all the nations under the sun. There was work to do, however, because Britain was at war with Spain and Gibraltar was under intermittent attack from Spanish gunboats and shore batteries. Miller recorded how in April 1797 they were 'Engaged by Spanish gunboats. They threw a number of shot into the garrison, killed several men, and drove the 42nd Regiment off the parade where they were at exercise,

Royal Foot Artillery Gunners. *(Philip Haythornthwaite)*

114

and knocked down several trees.'[2] Nevertheless, garrison duty at Gibraltar was tedious, and an expedition to Minorca in the autumn of 1798 was a welcome relief.

The expedition embarked under General Charles Stuart on 19 October landed on 7 November and had possession of the whole island eight days later. Stuart had overwhelmed the enemy by rapid movement and confidence to achieve a bloodless victory. For Miller what followed was

> the happiest time ... I ever had in the service; the people were so friendly with us. My master [he was an officer's servant at this time] and I lived with a family of Minorquins in this town, who were very fond of me.[3]

However, when the opportunity arose he volunteered for the expedition to Egypt and the chance of more action.

Miller spent a year sailing between Gibraltar and Tetuan, and then on to Malta under orders for Egypt. In Malta he succumbed to the temptations which ruined so many soldiers, when he and another man took an officer ashore:

> Very wet day, which caused us to go to a wine-house, where we got drunk. It rained four hours with such rapidity that it washed the cats and dogs from the street into the sea. I was nearly washed away when saving a cat when drunk. On our coming to the boat it was sunk with the quantity of rain that fell. It took us near night to clear the boat, after which we put to sea, but being both so very drunk we could not find our ship. A sergeant and a party of men were put in a boat to search for us, and took us on board prisoners, but when we got on board the officers took compassion on us being so wet and cold, they sent me to bed and gave me a bottle of rum.[4]

Miller learnt his lesson from this escapade.

In Egypt Miller, like Nicol, marched to Cairo after the victory at Alexandria and suffered the same conditions. 'Beginning of May. The hot winds began. We could scarcely bear our heads out of the tents. The Arabs frequently drop dead in the marketplace with it';[5] while 'The flies were so numerous that at times they darkened the air and appeared like a black cloud before us.'[6] Miller suffered from ophthalmia, a fever and a lump in his armpit (which sounds suspiciously like plague) during the campaign. He also found himself

Landings at Aboukir Bay. (*Author's collection*)

dwelling on the transience of life when he visited the graves of his fallen colleagues:

> I would reflect how dreadful it was to be cut off so suddenly and so neglectful as soldiers are in regard of religion ... for no sooner, perhaps, does he think of prayer than the drum beats or trumpets sound to arms – and how can he talk of forgiving his enemies when it is his whole duty to destroy them.[7]

In battle the artilleryman needed to stand by his guns. At Alexandria the French

> charged one of our batteries after our ammunition was done and would have killed every man. They gave some of the gunners shocking cuts, I was cut in both legs. But the gallant 42nd came to our assistance and killed every Frenchman that was in the battery ... We lost a great number, no less than 60 Artillerymen killed and wounded, but our loss was nothing to the loss of the enemy.[8]

116

Towards the end of the campaign part of the army was transported 7 miles to the west of Alexandria, and the artillery was ordered to bombard the island and castle of Marabout. There followed the hard work of getting the guns into position:

> We worked hard all night in getting our guns down and building a sand-bag battery. By daylight we had all ready, and opened on them with 12 guns and mortars, for about an hour. The enemy returned our fire very smartly, and made the grape and case shot fire among us, and rattle against our guns and wheels like showers of hailstones. I got a thump on my nose with a small stone which was struck by a shot, but we soon sunk [*sic*] three of their gun-vessels and disabled the other, and dismounted most of their guns on the battery. We then began to bombard the Castle ... we at last had the pleasure to see the castle fall to the ground, and we heard our army give three cheers.[9]

This success was crucial in setting up a two-pronged attack on Alexandria. As the guns threatened the city itself the French finally surrendered and the campaign was over.

Miller now returned briefly to Minorca. When the island was surrendered to Spain by the terms of the Peace of Amiens he sailed back to Gibraltar where he spent the next six years, initially very unhappily under the tyrannical rule of the Duke of Kent. This had horrendous implications for the gunners when several regiments mutinied:

> This was a horrid Christmas, for the night after Christmas, we were formed up against [the 25th regiment] who broke out in rebellion, and killed many of them. I was at a gun that was formed up close in front of them and expected every man of us would have been put to death. They frequently cried out 'Charge the Bugars,' 'Fire a volley at the Bugars.' I was more afraid than ever I was fighting against the French.[10]

Soon afterwards, the Duke made a hasty return to England.

Bombardier Miller, as he now was, had one more period of active service. He arrived in Lisbon in September 1808 and marched with the 6th regiment to Almeida, where they remained for two months before joining Sir John Moore's army for the operations which finally led to the retreat to Corunna. Like everyone else on that retreat he suffered from 'wet, cold, hunger, and want of rest'. At Villafranca we destroyed the remainder of waggons, stores, and ammunition, about 500 waggon loads, and even burned our knapsacks, so that we had only a few rounds of ammunition left. So now we were light enough, our backs almost bare, our bellies empty, and no shoes ... We got our guns over the snowy mountains with great difficulty, and two days after we met with fresh horses from Corunna.[11]

Like the cavalry, they had been shooting any horse that lost a shoe or went lame.

Royal Horse Artillery Gunner.
(*Philip Haythornthwaite*)

118

On 12 January 1809 Miller was sent into Corunna with a party to destroy everything belonging to the garrison, and the following day they marched about 5 miles to destroy two magazines, each with about 2,000 barrels of powder:

We had scarcely blown up the magazines before the enemy Riflemen came on us and began to fire, but we all made our escape and got safe to camp to the great surprise of our army, who thought we were all taken prisoners, and General Moore was heard to say those poor Artillerymen will all be killed or taken prisoner.

Royal Horse Artillery in action. (*Philip Haythornthwaite*)

During the battle on the 16th, Miller was with the guns attached to the piquets, whose task was to keep the French piquets at bay. A sharp exchange of fire developed, during which

> Generals Moore and Baird, who were standing by the gun which I commanded, came and looked over the wheel of the gun with a

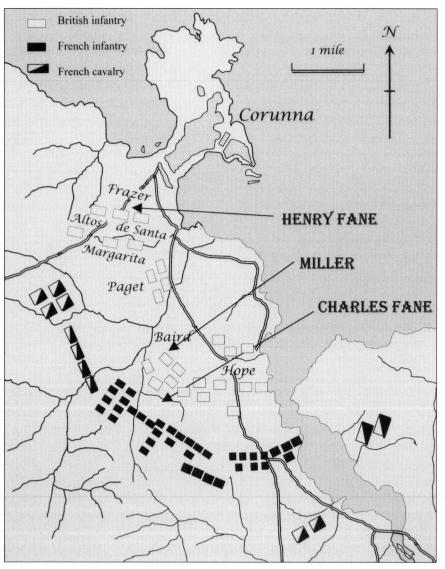

Battle of Corunna.

spy-glass and said to me 'don't fire any more, Artilleryman, for I don't think it will come to a general engagement today.' But he found to the contrary, for he was killed by a French cannon ball that evening and General Baird's arm was shot off.[12]

After holding the French at bay, the artillerymen were able to get their guns on board ship that night, and the next day the rest of the army embarked. Nine days later Miller found himself within sight of England for the first time in thirteen years.

Miller's fighting days were over but he remained with the artillery for another six years, on coastal command and then on recruiting duties. He also rose to the rank of sergeant. Then in December 1814 he fell from a ladder onto a cartwheel and fractured his skull. Three months later he was discharged with a pension of 1/6½d a day. He died in 1865 and was buried in Melbury Osmond, his birthplace eighty-eight years before.

Whereas Miller served with the Foot Artillery, Robert Macpherson Cairnes was an officer in the Royal Horse Artillery. All artillery

Battle of Corunna. (*Author's collection*)

officers were rigorously trained, having studied for between eighteen months and two years at the Royal Military Academy, Woolwich. Entry depended upon the recommendation of the Master General, and cadets were usually aged between 14 and 16. Cairnes' stepfather, Major-General William Cuppage, had sufficient influence to get young Robert into the Academy. Here he studied fortification, artillery, mathematics, drawing and French, with additional courses in chemistry. He was also taught the exercise of small arms and light field pieces, fencing and dancing.

Cairnes passed out in 1801, number 1106. This number was significant because commissions were not available for purchase in the artillery. Promotion was strictly by seniority, dependent upon the pass-out date from Woolwich, so that the ambitions of young officers were constantly frustrated by the presence of superannuated officers who were too old for service.

Cairnes arrived in Spain in April 1810, not to join Wellington but to become part of the British force commanded by General Graham in Cadiz. Since February Marshal Victor had been blockading this

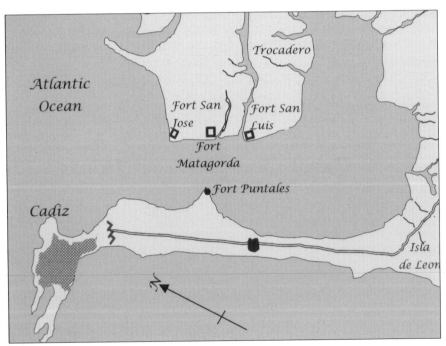

Map of Cadiz.

last Spanish stronghold and the Spanish had somewhat reluctantly sought British help, both military and naval.

For the first ten months the guns, under Major Duncan, performed a purely defensive role. At the beginning of 1811, however, Victor had to surrender some of his force to Marshal Soult, and the time seemed ripe for an Anglo-Spanish attack. Under the overall command of the inadequate General La Peña, an allied force landed at Algeciras and Tarifa. They trekked inland to draw Victor away from Cadiz so that the garrison could attack his lines. Then La Peña changed his mind and brought the allied forces back to Vejer de la Frontera, by way of flooded bridle-paths which posed particular problems for the guns. They now marched towards Conil and the beach track to San Petri.

On 5 March Graham's British force was holding the high ground at Barrosa. Graham realised the heights were crucial to the allied position but reluctantly obeyed La Peña's command to abandon them, whereupon the French seized the advantage afforded by this withdrawal, quickly driving off the small Spanish force which had replaced the British troops. Graham immediately retraced his route. With his 5,000 men he defeated 7,000 French, while 10,000 Spanish stood by as spectators.

Graham placed his artillery in the centre where Duncan and his ten guns soon opened a powerful battery which caused havoc to the French right, under General Laval. This allowed the British left to come up in some sort of order while the right held their ground. But it was a hard struggle. Of the twenty officers and 342 men with the guns fifty-four became casualties, including eight men killed. Graham wrote in his dispatch the next day: 'I owe too much to Major Duncan and the officers and corps of the Royal Artillery not to mention them in terms of the highest approbation. Never was artillery better served.'[13]

After Barrosa the siege returned to stalemate. It was finally raised on 24 August 1812, after Wellington's victory at Salamanca led the French to abandon Andalusia. By September Duncan's brigade of guns was at Seville. On the 29th the magazine exploded, killing Major Duncan and wounding second captains Cairnes and Cator.

By January 1813 Cairnes had recovered from his wounds and was at Vale da Mula, a few miles from Almeida, in acting command of Major Alexander Dickson's brigade. (Wellington had ignored seniority to place Dickson in command of the artillery.) There were several recurrent themes in Cairnes' letters to his stepfather. Forage

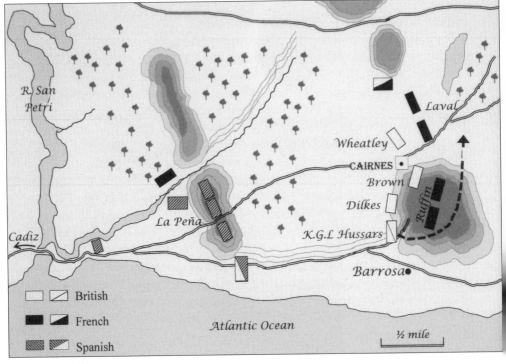

Battle of Barrosa.

for the horses was an ongoing concern; Cairnes realised that it would be impossible to launch a campaign until the spring grass came through. In March he moved to Penamacor, where there were stocks of hay sufficient to get his horses into condition but only a month later he was shocked by an order to surrender these same horses to the pontoon train. Although he obeyed, he could not hide his annoyance:

> After all the anxiety & trouble we have had since December last, it is almost too vexatious to bear that the Drivers and Horses should be slipped from under us, just when they have been brought (although we say it who should not) to as good discipline & condition as any other in the field.[14]

He was worried that replacement horses would not arrive in time to march with the army. The replacements did arrive as promised and Cairnes stoically accepted that his brigade had merely been in the wrong place at the wrong time.

Battle of Barrosa. (*Author's collection*)

Nevertheless, he now found himself with another problem:

I am getting my naked Drivers clothes here as well as I can. These lads were only three days in Lisbon when they were pushed up to the Army and unluckily fell to my lot. They leave England paid in advance, sell half their necessaries when lying at Portsmouth & the other half either at Lisbon or on the road (the Driver Officers never inspecting their kit). Thus they join a Brigade perfectly naked.

He felt some sympathy for them, however,

... considering the labour of taking care of two horses & their harness (& oftentimes of three) they are worse paid than any other troops ... By being with a Brigade, there is some hope of instilling into them the idea that they are soldiers, and when they find themselves looked after & treated precisely as the Gunners of the Brigade, they actually evince a difference.[15]

125

These were all practical problems which Cairnes was able to solve. Another issue which ran through the letters is the vexed problem of brevet promotion. Second captains, (an Ordnance rank) could not be rewarded with brevet promotion because they already held the army rank of captain, an injustice that rankled. In January 1813 Cairnes complained to his stepfather,

> I should like to get a Brevet Majority first, had not Lord Mulgrave [the Master General of the Ordnance] slapped the door to promotion in the faces of us poor Second Captains. Six of us are now commanding Troops & Brigades. The most distinguished mention in any dispatch would do us no good. Captains of the Line (who were not in the *Army* when some of *us were Captains*) get the Brevet for similar mention!![16]

The second captains sent a memorial to Wellington with the support of their senior officers. Wellington received it sympathetically, as did the Duke of York, who explained to Wellington that although he had felt it necessary to exclude second captains of Engineers and Artillery from the recommendation for brevet promotion that he made to his brother, he would now

> submit the Memorial for the gracious and favorable [*sic*] consideration of the Prince Regent, in order that your Lordship may in future be enabled to recommend for brevet rank such second Captains of Engineers and Artillery whose conduct shall merit your notice and protection.[17]

As the 1813 campaign got under way, Cairnes was attached to the 7th division under General Dalhousie. His two troops were armed with four light 6-pounder guns, one long 6-pounder and a heavy howitzer. The howitzer struck Cairnes as an unnecessary complication, requiring its own ammunition and carriage, but he was heartened by the excellent performance of his new horses and the promise that his old drivers would be returned to him. He also had the satisfaction of being told by Wellington's brother-in-law, General Pakenham, that his brigade was in excellent order.

Outmanoeuvred by Wellington, the retreating French finally made a stand at Vitoria on 21 June. Wellington attacked from four different directions and overwhelmed the enemy. The next day Lord Dalhousie published in a general order 'his high admiration of the conduct of the 1st brigade, and of Captain Cairnes' brigade of guns yesterday: nothing could surpass the steadiness & bravery of Men & Officers.

> "To Captain Cairnes the Officers & Men of the brigade of guns the Lieut. General offers his warmest acknowledgements for the readiness, steadiness, and excellence of their fire at all the different points where Captain Cairnes brought it to bear in the course of the day."[18]

In a letter home Cairnes described the events from his own perspective. While the 2nd and Portuguese brigades of the division lost their way,

> Our first brigade, however, were in their place & so (*nous nous flattons*) were we. The enemy were very strong (by guns in position) on their right which it fell to our column to attack & turn. [Their left flank had already been turned] ... the end was attained, and the French say they were perfectly unprepared to see our columns marching on their right. My guns were exposed to their cannonade from the right for a long time. I had then no troops of their's [*sic*] to direct my fire on & therefore fired on their guns (nine & I should think 12 Pdrs). We silenced & dislodged them, drawing their fire most conspicuously on ourselves *from* the first Brigade of our Division, which was not unnoticed nor unthanked by Lord Dalhousie to me.[19]

Cairnes' brigade was then detached to support the Spanish blockade of Pamplona but the appointment of Soult to command of the French and the consequent expectation of more action brought him back to the army. At Sorauren on 30 July he was again praised for the quality of his gunnery.

He continued to report events in the Pyrenees in his letters home, including an eye-witness account of the fall of San Sebastian, but the subject of brevet promotion was never far from his mind. In one letter he commented on a reference his stepfather had made to the generosity of Lord Mulgrave. He suspected this would take the form of money:

> *After* the service in the Peninsula, let those who are judged deserving of it, be thus rewarded. But whilst that service is going on, let us take our chance of the only *honourable* reward we can or ought to seek, that of Rank and Command.[20]

Cairnes finally obtained his brevet majority on 12 April 1814. Fourteen months later he was at Waterloo, second captain in Brevet Major Robert Bull's troop. They were originally posted in front of Mont St Jean Farm but at about midday they moved forward to add firepower to the defence of Hougoumont. They

'immediately came into action with spherical case shot with the intention of dislodging the Enemy's Infantry from the left of the small wood and the garden and the farm called Hougoumont adjoining, and at about 1,000 yards distance from our front, in which I have reason to believe we succeeded, for our Infantry were enabled to enter the wood.' The French, however, 'brought up six more Guns in our front, all of which were well served, and annoyed us considerably. It was from one of the flanking Guns that Major Cairnes was unfortunately killed, a few minutes after we got into our position.'[21]

Cairnes was buried on the battlefield, but a tablet was placed in Canterbury Cathedral,

Sacred to the Memory of Robert Macpherson Cairnes, Major of Royal Horse Artillery, who was taken from this sublunary scene June the 18th 1815, aged 30. Brief, but most noble, was his career, and his end was glorious, bravely asserting the cause of an

Artillery at Waterloo. (*Author's collection*)

injured monarch, he fell on the plains of Waterloo. His rare endowments, his high qualities, attractions of his character as son, as brother, and as friend, are indelibly impressed on the hearts of all who had the happiness of possessing his esteem, and who now feel the exquisite anguish inflicted by his early death. This humble monument erected by the hand of friendship, is a faithful, but very inadequate, testimony of affection, and grief which will never terminate till those who now deplore his loss shall join him in the blest realms of everlasting peace.

Researching Benjamin Miller and Robert Cairnes

Benjamin Miller's journal and Robert Cairnes' letters are invaluable sources of information for service with the guns. Miller started his diary in 1796 when he enlisted into the Royal Artillery. He reworked it sometime after 1813. The original diary was partially burnt, which is probably why he decided to produce a new manuscript but he also took the opportunity to add some extra details. Significantly, though, he did not cover the years 1804–08, which were the pages that had been destroyed by fire. This suggests that the later additions were facts he clearly remembered, whereas the extended lost period was beyond recall. The finished version is based on a contemporary record of his actions, thoughts and feelings which gives it the sense of immediacy sometimes lacking in retrospective memoirs. It also presents the perspective of a man in the ranks and few such diaries exist compared with those of officers.

There can be no doubt about the contemporaneous quality of Cairnes' letters. He was also a copious letter-writer, often sitting up late at night to 'catch the post', but he was equally eager to receive letters and often bewailed their failure to appear. As with Wheeler, there is a clear sense in these letters of a close-knit family, with every-one anxious to hear how everyone else is faring. What makes Cairnes' letters particularly interesting, though, is their focus on the minutiae of an artillery officer's life. In this respect, we are fortunate that the recipient was a fellow artillery officer whose interest in the day-to-day detail of commanding an artillery brigade could be assumed.

The National Archives are once again the main depository for documents pertaining to the service of both officers and men, but the Ordnance records have different references from Army documenta-tion. Benjamin Miller's discharge papers can be found in WO54 but give the expected information; that he enlisted aged 20, and was 5′ 7″ tall, with fair hair, dark eyes and a fair complexion. The muster rolls for the Royal Artillery are found in WO10, but give the same information as WO12. Another useful resource is WO69, which contains attestation papers and details of promotions, marriages and

Augustus Frazer of the Royal Horse Artillery. (*Philip Haythornthwaite*)

discharges or death. They are arranged by unit which in Miller's case was the 4th battalion of the Royal Foot Artillery.

Miller is also included in the General Service Medal Roll. He claimed the one clasp, Corunna, to which he was entitled when applications were invited in 1847 and seems to have been unaware that he could have added Egypt in 1850. He also became a local celebrity and his death was recorded in the local newspaper.

The National Archives also hold a *List of Officers of the Royal Regiment of Artillery 1716–June 1914* in three volumes. This makes a good starting point for researching officers. WO76 records the services of officers, 1770–1870, while WO54 (a portmanteau collection of Royal Artillery documents) contains pay-lists for officers and patents and warrants for appointment. Since all Royal Artillery officers had to attend the Royal Military Academy it is also worth contacting the Royal Military College, Sandhurst which holds the *Sandhurst Collection*. This includes cadets' records.

Notes

1. *The Adventures of Serjeant Benjamin Miller*, p. 4.
2. Ibid., p. 7.
3. Ibid., p. 13.
4. Ibid., p. 16.
5. Ibid., p. 20.
6. Ibid., p. 25.
7. Ibid., p. 19.
8. Ibid., p. 18.
9. Ibid., p. 25.
10. Ibid., p. 30.
11. Ibid., p. 34.
12. Ibid., p. 35.
13. *The Life of Lord Lynedoch*, p. 471.
14. *The Dickson Manuscripts*, Volume V, p. 880.
15. Ibid., p. 895.
16. Ibid., p. 833.
17. Ibid., p. 849.
18. Ibid., p. 914.
19. Ibid., p. 926.
20. Ibid., p. 1024.
21. Siborne, *Waterloo Letters*, pp. 188–9 (Major Bull's account).

Chapter Eight

THE CAREER OFFICER
Thomas Walker Chambers

There is a common, and justified, perception that officers of this period paid for their promotion. In fact, there were at least six different means by which a man might obtain a commission, and promotion might be achieved without purchase. In general, however, the popular perception is correct, and more officers were promoted 'with purchase' than by stepping into dead men's shoes or through particular recommendation. Such an officer was Thomas Walker Chambers of the 17th and 30th Foot.

Chambers was fortunate that he came from a wealthy background. As with many officers of the period, the money came from business ventures and although his maternal grandfather styled himself 'gentleman' and affected a coat of arms, this background was essentially what today we would categorise as middle-class. His grandfather, Philip Walker, owned herring-boats in Lowestoft and was co-founder of the Lowestoft porcelain factory. In addition, he had a financial interest in brick-making. When his only child, Mary, married John Chambers, they became partners in the herring industry, owning five boats between them, enough to give them a very comfortable living.

Thomas was born in 1781, the only surviving son of John and Mary Chambers. He was heir to both his father's and his grandfather's business interests but he chose a military career. When he was commissioned into the 17th Foot in 1799, aged 18, Britain had been at war with Revolutionary France for six years; a war apparently without end which promised more excitement to the young man than herring-boats, bricks and porcelain. The 17th Foot was stationed at Norwich in the summer of 1799, not far from Lowestoft, and, according to the August monthly return, had two vacant ensigncies. Chambers obtained one of these by purchase.

Two years later, when both battalions of the 17th were in Minorca, Chambers was promoted to lieutenant by seniority (so that there was no need to purchase the step in rank) and transferred from the first battalion, where he had been the senior ensign, to the second battalion, where he became the junior lieutenant. However, the negotiations which led to the Peace of Amiens (1802) promised peace. As a result, the second battalion left Minorca for Ireland, where it was disbanded, and Lieutenant Chambers found himself on half-pay.

This must have been frustrating for an ambitious young man who took his professional duties very seriously. The disappointment was short-lived, however. In May 1803 the peace collapsed with mutual accusations of bad faith. The British government, which had been busily reducing two-battalion regiments only a year before, now hurriedly augmented the strength of the army against the threat of a French invasion. One of the first regiments to obtain a second battalion was the 30th Foot. Chambers was noted in the September monthly return of the new battalion as 'not joined since appointed'. A month later he was with the battalion at Woodbridge, Suffolk, not far from his home in Lowestoft.

In January 1804 the two battalions of the 30th sailed to Ireland. The second battalion functioned as a feeder and training unit for the first and offered no chance of action. At the end of the year, though, Chambers was transferred to the first battalion which, late in 1805, formed part of Lord Cathcart's expedition to north Germany in support of the third coalition (Britain, Austria, Russia, Sweden). There was no military glory, however. The battle of Austerlitz on 2 December brought the coalition to an end when Napoleon comprehensively defeated the Austrians and Russians at 'The Battle of the Three Emperors'. By March the battalion was back in England. Two months later they were on board ship, sailing to India. Although some of the battalion experienced a brief period of service as marines, the battalion then settled into the tedium of life at Fort St George, Madras, where their main function was to support the ambitions of the East India Company.

In March 1807 Chambers, who was now senior lieutenant in the regiment, went with a detachment to Vellore under the command of Captain Thomas Jackson. While they were at Vellore Chambers was promoted to captain, paying the difference between the two commissions because there were no deaths in the regiment to create a vacancy. In October he also quarrelled with Jackson, seriously enough to be court-martialled, and in November he was suspended from rank and pay for three months. Although the details of the charges have been lost, subsequent evidence suggests that he was accused of insubordination and was cleared of all but the most minor misdemeanour. Nevertheless, the matter rankled because he later challenged Jackson to a duel (against the Articles of War). No blood was shed and it seems that Jackson then apologised for whatever had led to the court martial.

This might have been the end of the matter but rumours circulated around the mess that Chambers had apologised to Jackson, and not the other way about. Whatever his virtues, and there is testimony to suggest they were manifold, Chambers was clearly not the man who could tolerate a slur on his honour. In company with his friend, Lieutenant Nicholson, he requested Major Maxwell to set matters straight by informing the mess that it was Jackson who had apologised. Maxwell's refusal dramatically affected Chambers' career. Nicholson now added fuel to the fire by claiming that if Maxwell did not scotch the rumours there would be another duel and blood would be shed. By this time Chambers and Nicholson were at odds with nearly all their brother officers and General Wilkinson (lieutenant-colonel in the regiment) decided to intervene. In July 1809 he placed them both on a charge and then offered them the chance to be released from arrest if they resigned from the regiment, with the promise of a recommendation. Both agreed, but only Chambers actually signed the resignation and received a year's absence of leave to return to Europe and find another regiment. Nicholson refused to sign anything until he had received the promised recommendation, thus indicating that he did not trust the senior officers to keep their word. As a result, he was charged with ungentlemanly conduct, in that he had reneged on an agreement, and the previous charge that he had tried to incite a duel was also resurrected.

Although Chambers was in Madras by this time, preparing to sail to Europe in command of a detachment of invalids, he was summoned back to Trichinopoly, where the 1/30th was now stationed, as a prosecution witness. In fact, far from supporting the prosecution case, he undermined it by implying that the other main prosecution witness was guilty of perjury. Then he returned to Madras, and on to Europe. As for Nicholson, he was eventually cleared of the second charge, on the grounds that he had every right to see the recommendation before he signed a resignation. He was found guilty of actually saying that blood would be spilt, but the sentence was merely a reprimand, which took the form of a letter. Obviously the court was sympathetic to the prisoner on both counts, but it is also possible that Chambers' testimony had raised some doubt about the prosecution case.

Chambers should now have been looking for another regiment. He moved quickly, but in a different direction. He left India in April 1810. In July a detachment of reinforcements, under the command of an ensign, left the regimental depot in Wakefield for Cadiz, where the 2/30th was part of the defending force. When the detachment arrived in September Chambers was in command. At what point he took command is unclear. He did not travel to Wakefield because the depot returned him as absent with leave. He may have visited the regimental agent in London, found out what was happening and taken the opportunity to join the second battalion to which, as a junior captain, he properly belonged.

This was a momentous decision for a career officer. In India there was no action and the only escape was sickness, which would bring an officer back to Europe on leave for recovery of health. Otherwise, the first battalion held on to all its officers, whatever their position within their rank. The second battalion was on active service and represented an ambitious young man's best chance of distinguishing himself. Nor did he have long to wait. Within days of his arrival in Cadiz he found himself once more on board ship as the 2/30th sailed to Lisbon, preparatory to joining Wellington's Peninsular army.

A march up-country from the Portuguese capital brought the 2/30th to the Lines of Torres Vedras, where the battalion joined the 5th division, under General James Leith. The Lines proved an effective defensive measure, and although initially Marshal Masséna probed their strength with the hope of breaching them, he eventually acknowledged that he had been outmanoeuvred and retreated to Santarém. While the French went hungry in Santarém, Wellington's Anglo-British army enjoyed reasonable supplies behind the Lines. For the officers this was a period of relative pleasure: dinners with fellow officers, walking and shooting expeditions, visits to Lisbon and other places of interest. Such entertainment is detailed in the journal of the adjutant of the 2/30th, Lieutenant William Stewart, and there is no reason to believe that Chambers did not share in these agreeable activities. The tensions of the first battalion were far behind him. Only once did he have a recorded difference of opinion with an officer of the second battalion, and that lay in the future. Furthermore, after the departure of Lieutenant-Colonel Minet to Lisbon to act as president of a court martial, followed by his promotion to the general list, command of the battalion devolved on Major Alexander Hamilton who, like Chambers, was a dedicated career officer, both popular and efficient. The two men were to serve together until Waterloo. It is not clear whether Minet or Hamilton appointed Chambers to command the light company. Either way, it was recognition of his talent, since the light company, as one of the two flank companies, was a particularly prestigious appointment.

The relaxed time behind the Lines came to an end on 6 March 1811, when Masséna left Santarém without warning. The adjutant received orders to have the battalion ready to march at the shortest notice, and there followed a long pursuit northwards, and then east towards the Spanish border. Every town or village they passed through was marked by evidence of French depredation as an army convinced of its superiority vented its frustration on the country it was being forced to abandon.

On 3 April the 5th division finally came close to the enemy. (Up to this point the light and 3rd divisions had seen most of the action as Wellington's van encountered the French rear.) At Sabugal the division was required to storm its way into the town while the light and 3rd divisions directly attacked the French second corps under General Reynier. Some confusion of position and orders meant these last two divisions, particularly the light, had a fierce fight on their hands. At a crucial moment, however, the 5th division crossed the Agueda and drove the French right from the heights they occupied. Their reward was the meal that the French were forced to abandon.

Masséna crossed into Spain and established himself in Salamanca, while the Anglo-Portuguese took up a position along the border, from Nave d'Haver to Obispo. Not all the French were out of Portugal, however, and Masséna's attempt to relieve the garrison at Almeida led to the action at Fuentes de Oñoro. The 5th division was on the extreme left of Wellington's position, at Fort Concepcion, posted to block the direct route to Almeida. Protected by a deep ravine to their front, they merely engaged in some light skirmishing with the tirailleurs of Reynier's second corps. Nevertheless, Chambers as commander of the light company was engaged in this limited action.

Once Masséna had withdrawn to Salamanca, where he was replaced by Marshal Marmont, the Anglo-Portuguese army took up more extended positions along the border. Wellington's objective was the Spanish fortress of Ciudad Rodrigo, but it was January 1812 before he began the investment. Although officers and men of the 2/30th volunteered for engineering and artificer duties, there is no way of knowing whether Chambers was one of them. The number of survivors who claimed a bar for Ciudad Rodrigo on their General Service Medals suggests that the 2/30th provided the largest contingent from the battalions of the 5th division, so it is possible that he was involved.

After the fall of the northern border fortress, Badajoz became Wellington's next goal. Here, for the first time since the Battle of Buçaco in September 1810 the 5th division played a crucial part in the action. While the light and 4th divisions stormed the breaches and the 3rd division escaladed the castle, the 5th division escaladed the bastion of San Vincente. The assault took place on 6 April and was planned to start at ten o'clock. The 5th division, however, were misdirected by the officer guiding the ladder party and it was nearly midnight when they finally raised their ladders. By this time, the 3rd division had successfully escaladed the castle, where they still remained, and the light and 4th divisions had taken heavy casualties at the breaches.

The first men of the 5th division up the ladders at San Vincente were the light companies of the 2nd brigade, the 2/4th, 2/30th and 2/44th, followed by a company of Black Brunswick Jägers. Inevitably, they took the heaviest casualties. Only one officer of the 30th was killed, Major George Grey in temporary command, but the most seriously wounded officer was Captain Chambers. He was out of action until August, thus missing the victory at Salamanca in which the 5th division again played a notable part, having been the first division into Badajoz, and the triumphant entry into Madrid. He finally rejoined the battalion on the march north to Burgos, another challenging stronghold in French hands.

The 5th division acted as a covering force during the unsuccessful investment of Burgos. By October Wellington was in retreat. On the 25th the 5th division was charged with holding a position at Villamuriel so that the rest of the army could withdraw safely. The light company, in its skirmishing role and under Chambers'

Badajoz, the escalade of San Vincente bastion. (*Author's collection*)

command, played an important part in holding the French at bay for the whole day.

The conditions of the retreat worsened as the weather deteriorated. The French pursued relentlessly; men, women and children fell by the wayside; supplies broke down. Yet amidst the chaos the 30th preserved reasonable order; in the worst three days of the retreat they lost one man dead, five taken prisoner, and three missing. Indeed, the forty-five lost during the whole retreat, which included twenty killed or missing at Villamuriel, suggests that the commanding officer, Hamilton, now lieutenant-colonel, and his senior officers effectively preserved discipline.

By this time, though, the battalion had been seriously weakened by its losses during the past two years. It had arrived behind the Lines in October 1810 nearly 700 strong; by December only 243 NCOs and men were fit for duty. As a result, the fit men were reorganised into four companies and formed into a provisional battalion with the

Thomas Walker Chambers.
(*John Macdonald*)

similarly under-strength 2/44th. The weak men were sent back to England. Chambers remained in the Peninsula and must have been hoping for more action, but the powers that be disliked provisional battalions, and the remnants of the two battalions were sent home in June 1813.

This proved a brief respite, although it did enable Chambers to take some leave, his first since he joined the 30th. It may also have been at this time his portrait was painted because he wears the bugle badge of the light company. By January 1814 the battalion was in Flanders as part of a force under General Sir Thomas Graham, who, in alliance with the Prussians, hoped to take Antwerp from the French. At this point a young gentleman volunteer, Edward Neville Macready joined the 30th and, as was customary, was attached to the light company. His journal makes several references to Chambers.

For example, as Macready candidly admitted in the privacy of his journal, when he first came under cannonade from the French, he was very afraid:

> We had a number of tyros besides myself, and I saw enough to convince me that a young man must not be judged too harshly of for a little timidity on his first essay in arms. My Captain, Chambers, made this remark, and pointed out a young fellow who seemed somewhat alarmed, and who has since behaved with distinguished gallantry.[1]

Chambers may have understood the fear experienced by a tyro, but he did not tolerate the adolescent bumptiousness which is implicit in Macready's journal. It is not clear on what grounds he took the young man to task, but Macready nursed resentment thereafter.

Graham's expedition was not a success. The commander's strategy was stronger than his senior officers' execution, particularly at the failed attack on Bergen-op-Zoom in which the 2/30th was not involved (although the Peninsular veterans thought they should have been). However, Napoleon's first abdication, in April, brought the campaign to an end. The battalion remained in Belgium, although Chambers returned to England with a party of men who were to be discharged.

At this point he purchased his next promotion, to major. The vacancy was caused by the return to England of Captain Thomas Roberts, who had been a prisoner in France since 1805. Roberts immediately received a step in rank, but he also purchased a lieutenant-colonelcy in De Rolls regiment. Although Chambers was not the senior captain in the 30th, he had the money, was on the spot and undoubtedly had the support of his commanding officer, having been the only captain Hamilton kept with him in Portugal when the six companies returned to England.

Major Chambers returned to Belgium in March, days after Napoleon's return to France from Elba. He was now the junior major in the regiment yet, when the 2/30th, in Halkett's British brigade of the 3rd division, went into action against the French at Quatre Bras (16 June 1815), Chambers found himself in command. Hamilton was wounded quite early on; Major Bailey, taken by surprise at the speed of Napoleon's advance, was still in Brussels; and Major Vigoureux was in detached command of a light infantry unit. Macready makes clear that Chambers' skill and determination were much in evidence.

Towards the close of the battle, the French

made a faint charge on ours and some other battalions, but being uniformly repulsed, retired, and we occupied our former ground. We now descended a slope towards our right in the direction of a deep ravine, across which the Royal Scots and ourselves drove a heavy body of infantry after a severe fire. The enemy was retiring from the [Bossu] wood, and the Guards pressing them very closely. A retrograde movement was perceptible along their whole line, and it was performed in beautiful style; their columns and skirmishers kept their alignment and distances as if on parade ... Major Chambers of ours, was pushing on with two companies towards a house in our front, and I joined him with as many of the Light Infantry as I could collect. We rushed into the courtyard, but were repulsed. He re-formed us in the orchard, directed the men how to attack, and it was carried in an instant by battering open the doors and ramming the muskets into the windows. We found 140 wounded and some excellent beer in the house.[2]

Two days later the battalion was in the centre of the allied position at Waterloo and once again Chambers found himself in command. Hamilton was absent, incapacitated by his serious leg wound, and both Bailey and Vigoureux were wounded early in the battle. He seems to have exercised command with his usual competence, particularly when, towards the end of the battle, a moment of panic led to a scrabbling retreat under heavy French artillery fire:

There was a hedge to our rear, to which we were ordered to move, as some cover from the fire. As we descended the declivity, the enemy thought we were flying, and, according to their invariable custom, turned a trebly furious cannonade upon us. Shot, shell, and grape came like a hurricane through the square, and the hurly burly of those moments can never be erased from my memory ... At this instant the two regiments on our right [the 33rd and 2/69th] rushed amongst us in frightful confusion, and our men passed the hedge at an accelerated pace. The exertions of the officers were rendered to no avail by the irresistible pressure, and, as crying in rage and shame, they seized individuals to halt them, they were themselves hurried on by the current. Such a jumble of curses, screams, sobs and laughter as arose amongst our mob. At this moment someone huzzaed, we all joined, and the men halted. Major Chambers ordered me to dash out with our light bobs and grenadiers, while the regiment marched up to the hedge and reformed.[3]

What happened next is uncertain. His brother-in-law later met some wounded men of the 30th at Yarmouth and they described how Chambers was shot as he desperately galloped his horse into the safety of a square. Another version has him standing with a group of officers, each congratulating himself on having survived the battle. Chambers hoped for promotion to lieutenant-colonel. Moments later he was killed by a stray shot. The first version does not fit what was happening at the time he was killed. The second is the distant recollection of an elderly man. More convincing, and ironic, is the account of Chambers' fellow officer, Captain Arthur Gore, written two years after the battle:

> About half past six [probably a little later] at the moment he was declaring 'that he had hitherto escaped unhurt, and that he was too small to be hit,' he received a ball through the heart, from a tirailleur of the guards, and instantly expired.[4]

Macready, who put Chambers' death some time after seven o'clock but gave no details of the circumstances, recorded how 'his friend Nicholson threw himself on the body and sobbed aloud, "My friend – my friend!"' (Nicholson had joined the second battalion from India in 1813). Macready also described how 'Two officers of ours were not on terms; the one saw the other behaving gallantly, he ran up to him and cried, "Shake hands, and forgive all that has passed; you're a noble fellow."'[5] This is believed to be how Chambers and Macready were reconciled, even though Macready chose to write in the third person, possibly on account of his embarrassment at his youthful arrogance.

There is no doubt that Chambers' death was mourned by more than just Nicholson. Gore wrote:

> I cannot remain deaf to the voice of friendship and worth. Of that number, there is no-one more worthy 'of the voice of praise' than my friend and companion in arms, Major T.W. Chambers ... He was an active, zealous, and intelligent officer, and a great loss to his regiment, both as a soldier, and as a gentleman.[6]

Even Macready, whose dealings with Chambers had not been easy, conceded that he was 'A strange mortal, but an admirable soldier. My forbearance does not proceed from any regard to the ridiculous aphorism *de mortuis nil nisi bonum*, but from respect for the memory of a man whose valour and abilities were undeniable.'

Chambers, like Cairnes, was buried on the battlefield. As his memorial in St Margaret's Church, Lowestoft puts it: 'after highly distinguishing himself in Europe and India for 18 years [he] fell gloriously fighting at the memorable Battle of Waterloo on the 18th day of June in the 34th year of his life.' A career soldier in every sense of the word, he had chosen a path that took him away from a comfortable life in a Suffolk town. He found a vocation that enabled him to demonstrate qualities of the highest order. And, in the rather strange mores of his time, he 'died the death that every soldier looks for'.[7]

Researching Thomas Walker Chambers

In some ways, researching the career of an officer is more straight-forward than researching a man in the ranks, particularly if his regiment is not known. The starting point is the Army Lists, which have been produced annually since 1754 (there are some earlier ones). There is a name index at the back of each volume which enables an individual officer's regiment to be identified, although it is important to allow for variant spelling of surnames, as was seen with Andrew Hartley. Once the officer has been located in a particular regiment it is a simple matter to follow his career, as Chambers' was through the 17th Foot, half-pay and the 30th Foot, because the lists include promotions, transfers and other changes. Complementing the Army Lists are the monthly returns (WO17) which trace the officer's service on a monthly basis. Chambers' circumstances from the time he went on detachment to Vellore until he arrived in Cadiz were established by consulting these returns, and the proceedings for Nicholson's court martial (WO71). These papers make clear that Chambers signed a resignation, which suggests that joining the second battalion was always his intention.

Officers are more likely to figure in their fellow-officers' journals, letters and memoirs than men in the ranks (unless they are unusual characters like Tom Plunket). Macready, the son and brother of actors, had a developed sense of the dramatic, so his presentation of

143

Chambers is particularly vivid. His respect for Chambers tells us much about the man, for Macready knew how to bear a grudge. Similarly, Nicholson's grief and Gore's elegiac comments suggest a man who was both loved and respected within the battalion.

Because officers were not discharged but sold their commissions, there is no equivalent of WO97, which creates problems for the researcher who wants to investigate an officer's life beyond his military career. Parish records will help if his geographical origins are known. Otherwise, progress may be dependent on luck.

In the case of Chambers, an enquiry to the museum of the Queen's Lancashire Regiment (which incorporated the 30th as its senior regiment) was passed on to me. John Macdonald, a direct descendant of one of Chambers' five sisters, generously shared all he knew of the family, as well as giving me a copy of his portrait. This information established the link to the herring trade and the porcelain works, and also revealed that Philip Walker left bequests to all his grand-children, which may well have proved useful to his grandson in furthering his career. Perhaps most interesting was the letter written after Chambers' death by his brother-in-law, John Rush, which not only includes the version he was told in Yarmouth but also confirms that Chambers purchased his majority. Rush advised the family to reclaim the money. Another interesting document was Chambers' will, written in India in 1808. Wills are always a useful line of research.

Knowing that Chambers came from Lowestoft took me to the Lowestoft Records Office where, with the help of the staff, I discovered a wealth of information about his family background. Books written by antiquarians, census returns for 1821 and 1831, as well as the parish records of St Margaret's Church all contributed to an understanding of Chambers' social background and status. By combining this understanding with all that is known about his military career, it is possible to gain a clear impression of this 'strange mortal' but 'admirable soldier'.

Notes
1. The unpublished journal of Edward Neville Macready, chapter 4.
2. Ibid., chapter 10.
3. Ibid., chapter 12.
4. Craan (trans. Gore), *An Historical Account of the Battle of Waterloo*, pp. 92–3.
5. Macready, chapter 12.
6. Craan/Gore, p. 92.
7. Macready, chapter 12.

Chapter Nine

FAMILY AT WAR
The Fanes of Fulbeck

As the sun rose on the hills around Vitoria on 21 June 1813 three brothers awaited the orders which would take them into action against the French. Two of them were experienced senior officers, a major-general and a lieutenant-colonel. The third, an inexperienced ensign, was about to go into battle for the first time. If we should wonder what had brought these three men into the army, the eldest of them 34 with nearly twenty years' experience, the youngest only 18, a visit to Fulbeck church in Lincolnshire will provide the answer.

On the north wall of the church are memorials to seven of the sons of the Honourable Henry Fane, brother of the 9th Earl of Westmorland, and Ann Batson, a Dorset heiress. On another wall is an elaborate memorial to the eighth son. One of them could have resided at Fulbeck Hall and enjoyed an easy social life after the death of his father in 1802. Instead, all eight dedicated themselves to a life of occupation and service. As well as the three soldiers, there was a clergyman, a Royal Naval lieutenant who died in Barbados aged 21, a banker who also served as a Member of Parliament, and two civil servants, one of whom was with the Bengal Civil Service. This was a family with a highly-developed sense of duty.

The first son to join the army was the eldest, Henry. Born in 1778, he is recorded in 1792 as cornet in the 6th Dragoon Guards, aged 14, although it is unlikely that they ever saw him. He first appears in the Army List in 1793, having been appointed lieutenant in the 55th Foot in September 1792. It may be assumed that both these commissions were purchased. In 1793 he was in Ireland, serving as aide-de-camp to the Lord Lieutenant, who just happened to be his cousin. He was also promoted captain-lieutenant (that is, senior lieutenant) in the 4th (Royal Irish) Dragoon Guards, rising to major in 1795 and a young lieutenant-colonel at the beginning of 1797. Again, money probably helped his progress.

Henry was back in England with his regiment by 1794, when he spent nine months recruiting, an activity brought to an end by his

Memorials in Fulbeck Church.

promotion to major. Apart from some periods of leave, one specif-
ically in 1804 so that he could attend 'the Imperial Parliament' (he
was Member of Parliament for Lyme Regis), he remained with the
Royal Irish until 1804, by which time he was owner of Fulbeck Hall.
There seems to have been no temptation to abandon his military
career, however. In 1804 he was appointed lieutenant-colonel with
the 1st Dragoon Guards and honoured with the additional appointment of aide-de-camp to the king and the rank of colonel in the army.
Up to this point, though, he had seen no active service.

In 1808 he was appointed brigadier general to a brigade consisting
of the 1/45th, 5/60th and 2/95th, the last two being rifle battalions.
This brigade was part of an expedition to Portugal (originally
intended for South America) under the command of Sir Arthur
Wellesley. Among Fane's troops was Benjamin Harris, who so clearly
remembered the discomforts of the campaign. Not that the general
suffered any less than the common soldier in those burning August
days as the army landed at Mondego Bay and then moved against the
French. An engineer, George Landmann, coming across General Fane

Henry Fane.
(*Author's collection*)

147

near Alcobaça, noticed that his underlip was so dry and inflamed that the blood was running down his chin.

Rifleman Harris encountered Henry Fane soon after they landed, while

> posted sentinel between two hedges. A short time later General Fane came up and cautioned me to be alert. 'Remember, sentinel,' he said, 'we are now near an active enemy; therefore, be careful here, and mind what you are about.'[1]

At the first action in the Peninsular War to involve British troops, Fane's brigade was on the left of the centre column, which marched directly against the French while a left and a right column came at them obliquely. Fane sent his riflemen forward to engage the French tirailleurs. As the French withdrew to higher ground, the brigade began to ascend the heights well to the left, the riflemen still warmly engaged with the tirailleurs, 'rooting them out' as Captain Leach of the 95th described it. When they reached the summit and attacked the French right, they were rudely driven back. Twice they returned and twice they were counter-charged. At the fourth attempt they gained a lodgement, just as Ferguson's column appeared on the left and convinced General Delaborde, in command, that it was time to withdraw.

While Marshal Junot marched up from Lisbon, having finally recognised that he needed to deal with the British but moving too late to help Delaborde, Wellesley kept close to the coast, awaiting the landing of two more brigades. On 21 August, four days after the action at Roliça, the two armies went into battle at Vimeiro. Wellesley had placed his troops on high ground, including Fane and Anstruther's brigades in front of Vimeiro itself. Fane still had his riflemen, although the 45th had been replaced by the 1/50th. Piquets of riflemen were holding a forward position. They were the first to come into contact with the advancing French, and were soon driven back. As the French columns continued their advance, the men of Fane and Anstruther's brigades were desperate to charge:

> But General Fane restrained their impetuosity. He desired them to stand fast, and keep their ground. 'Don't be too eager, men,' he said, as coolly as if we were on a drill parade in Old England. 'I don't want you to advance just yet. Well done, 95th!' he called out, as he galloped up and down the line. 'Well done 43rd, 52nd,

and well done all! If I live I'll not forget your conduct today. They shall hear of it in England, my lads!'

At this moment [a certain private] Brotherwood rushed up to the general and presented him with the green feather that he had torn out of the cap of a French light-infantry soldier he had killed. 'God bless you, general,' he said, 'and wear this for the sake of the 95th.'

The general took the feather and stuck it in his cocked hat. The next minute he gave the word to charge, and down came the whole line through a tremendous fire of cannon and musketry[2]

and swept the French from that part of the field.

After the victory at Vimeiro Wellesley was superseded by two senior generals and then summoned with them to England, to face an enquiry into the terms of the Convention of Cintra. Henry Fane remained in Portugal, and marched with Sir John Moore into Spain. During this frustrating campaign, which ended with the retreat to Corunna, he was joined by his next brother, Charles, three years his junior, who was lieutenant-colonel of the 2/59th. Henry now commanded a brigade of the 1/38th, 79th and 1/82nd in Fraser's 3rd division while the 1/59th was in Sir James Leith's brigade of Sir John Hope's 2nd division.

Charles Fane, like his brother, went into the army young but it was not until the end of 1797, when he was 18, that he began regular service as lieutenant in the Coldstream Guards. Before this he studied military science in Germany. His first experience of active campaigning came in 1801 when he distinguished himself during the Egypt campaign. Two years later he was serving as adjutant with his regiment and then in 1805 he was appointed lieutenant-colonel of the 2/59th.

Charles Fane's battalion was one of those which experienced the horrors of the retreat to Corunna, although the losses taken while on the march were lower than many other battalions. This may be due to the lieutenant-colonel, who was a strict disciplinarian. The 59th had white facings to their uniform and were known, like most similar regiments, as 'The Lilywhites'. In their case the name was justified because during the retreat Charles insisted that the men keep their facings clean with frequent applications of pipe-clay, a clever device to remind the men that they were soldiers.

Charles Fane.
(Author's collection)

At the battle on 16 January 1809 that ended Moore's campaign the 59th were posted near the village of Palavea, acting as a reserve. Towards the end of the action Hope sent them in support of two other battalions, the 3/1st and 2/81st, which had taken heavy losses and were running low on ammunition. Their arrival forced the French to retire from this part of the field but not before their lieutenant-colonel suffered a dangerous head wound, a section of skull being carried away.

In contrast, Henry Fane in Fraser's division, which was posted close to Corunna on the ridge of Santa Margarita guarding the road down to the town, saw little action. A probing cavalry attack was easily seen off.

Charles Fane would not return to the Peninsula until 1813 but Henry, having come through three battles unscathed, was with Wellesley's army throughout the 1809 campaign which began with the crossing of the Douro in May. He was now in command of the second cavalry brigade, comprising the 3rd Dragoon Guards and

4th Dragoons. At Talavera he had 1,000 men under his command. On 28 July, the second day of the battle, in sweltering temperature sufficient to set the grass ablaze a French infantry advance was charged by Anson's cavalry brigade (23rd Light Dragoons and KGL 1st Hussars). Fane's heavy cavalry was in support. Anson's charge soon ran into trouble when the cantering horses, probably as excited as their riders, encountered a dry watercourse, up to 6 feet deep in places and 12 feet wide. Fane resisted the temptation to follow Anson, the wisdom of which is borne out by the comparative casualty figures, fifteen for his brigade against 244 in Anson's. As at Vimeiro, he demonstrated his ability to hold eager men in check, for they would undoubtedly have charged, given the opportunity, and have shared the fate of Anson's regiments. Furthermore, by keeping to their ground they deterred a renewed French advance.

In the spring of 1810 Fane was attached to Hill's 2nd division, in command of the 13th Light Dragoons and four Portuguese cavalry regiments. Hill's division was detached at Portalegre to prevent a French incursion into the Alentejo while the rest of the army was further north. In June Hill crossed the Tagus at Vila Velha to frustrate French manoeuvres that threatened the main Anglo-Portuguese army. From this point until the battle of Buçaco on 27 September Hill was fully engaged in watching the French, using Fane's cavalry for outpost work. After Buçaco and the withdrawal to the Lines of Torres Vedras Fane was sent across the Tagus to watch Masséna at Santarém. If he discovered that Masséna was building boats for the purpose of putting a pontoon bridge across the Tagus, he was instructed by Wellington (as he now was) to destroy them with rockets. The rocket attack failed, but the presence of allied cavalry on the other side of the river seems to have deterred Masséna from attempting a crossing.

Fane had received this letter of instruction from Wellington on 15 November. The salutation, 'My dear Fane', was indicative of Wellington's warm feelings for him. Otherwise it would have been 'Dear General', or even just 'General'.

Henry's health was failing, however, and at the end of the year he returned to England on sick leave. His departure was undoubtedly regretted by Wellington; in 1812, in reply to a letter from Lord Bathurst, Secretary of State for War and the Colonies, he wrote: 'I should be very glad to have the assistance of General Fane, but we have no vacancy at present in the cavalry.' The situation he had previously held was now filled by a lieutenant-general, who could not be replaced by a mere major-general. Nevertheless, at the end of the year, when Wellington was arranging the removal of some of his inadequate cavalry generals, he stressed that the only replacement he wanted was Henry Fane.

Thus at the beginning of 1813 not only did Henry return to command the heavy cavalry attached to Hill's division (3rd Dragoon Guards, 1st Royal Dragoons, a regiment of Portuguese dragoons and Captain Bean's troop, RHA) but Charles also considered himself fit enough to rejoin the 2/59th. He had had four extended periods of sick leave since his return to England, indicative of the seriousness of his wound. His battalion had arrived in Cadiz in September 1812, and he finally joined them in March 1813. He had been advised to have his skull trepanned but such was his desire to be with his regiment that he said he would defer the operation until he returned to England. Reunited with his battalion, he was also in command of the sixth of his seven brothers, Mildmay, who had been commissioned

Mildmay Fane.
(*Author's collection*)

152

into the 59th as an ensign in June 1812, and joined the second battalion in the Peninsula at the same time as his brother, and their cousin, George Fane, newly promoted to lieutenant. A month later they were at Santarém, part of Wellington's army.

Henry's arrival seems to have been welcomed by the cavalry because he had a good reputation for competence, although he was also a strict disciplinarian like his brother. For instance, the *Journal* of the Royal Dragoons gives the example of four men tried by court martial under Fane for assaulting and robbing a Spanish muleteer. Two were acquitted, which suggests that his severity was applied discriminately, but the other two were sentenced to 400 and 900 lashes, although the full sentence was not inflicted. On the other hand, he had some understanding of the effects of boredom on high-spirited young gentlemen. After a rather unfortunate practical joke, which involved a drunken officer being stripped naked by Spanish women, he summoned each participant individually in order to deliver a lecture on 'conduct unbecoming an officer and a gentleman'.

Henry was the first of the three brothers to see action. On 26 May, his brigade and Victor Alten's brigade of light cavalry caught up with General Villatte's infantry at Salamanca. Both brigades went in pursuit; Alten used the bridge to cross the Tormes, and Henry, the Santa Marta fords. When they caught up with the French, however, they became tentative, failing to push home their charges. Henry used his horse artillery battery to some effect and both brigades picked up stragglers but after 5 miles Wellington caught up with them and ordered them to abandon the pursuit. Henry, it seems, was reluctant to sacrifice his men unnecessarily and probably welcomed the order. The men of the Royals, however, felt that an opportunity for glory had been wasted.

Wellington continued his two-pronged advance which was inexorably driving the French towards the Pyrenees until on 20 June the enemy finally stopped retreating and took up a position at Vitoria. When the action began the next day Hill's division attacked from the Heights of Puebla, which left no role for the attached cavalry other than to ride along the valley in rather detached support. Charles and Mildmay, however, in the 5th division, were part of General Graham's attack on Gamarra Mayor. The village was captured but the bridge beyond proved an impassable obstacle. Robinson's brigade, in which the 2/59th served, exhausted itself in

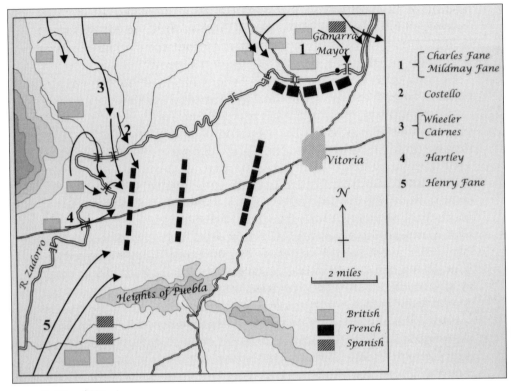

Battle of Vitoria.

three separate attacks. Eventually, a stalemate developed as both sides trained their guns on this narrow front. As a result, the 5th division lost thirty-eight officers and 515 men (while the French lost the same number of officers and 558 men).

Among the casualties was Lieutenant-Colonel Charles Fane who

> had his leg and part of his thigh carried off, but survived the wound some days. He wrote to some of his relations after he had received his wounds. His last moments were easy and quiet. He was buried at Vittoria [sic], the scene of his latest glory and his death,

his passing being noted as the loss of 'one of the most promising officers in the service'.[3] He was aged 32.

For Mildmay the summer of 1813 was a distressing period. Not only did he lose his brother at Vitoria but on 31 August his cousin George, with whom he had joined the regiment, was killed at the

154

assault of San Sebastian. Their closeness is indicated by George leaving all his effects to his cousin. (Charles left his to his servants.)

Both Henry and Mildmay, who was promoted to lieutenant in September, remained in the Peninsula until the end of the war. For Henry this involved covering Hill at the blockade of Bayonne in January 1814, and then commanding his cavalry at Orthes, Aire and Toulouse. Mildmay's General Service Medal has clasps for San Sebastian and the Nive, as well as Vitoria. Henry was also awarded the Army Gold Cross, having already received a Corunna Gold Medal.

The Peninsular War might now be over, but there was one more campaign to come. During the interim between Napoleon's abdication and return from Elba, Henry was appointed colonel of the 23rd Light Dragoons and then of the 4th Dragoons, and was also appointed Inspector of Cavalry. At the news of Napoleon's return he was placed in command of the Sussex (Military) division. He was then moved to the Centre division, to deal with civil unrest in the Midlands. Mildmay, meanwhile, acquired a captaincy in the 44th in March 1815 and joined the battalion in Flanders in time for the Waterloo campaign.

The 2/44th were with Picton's 5th division, in a brigade commanded by Sir Denis Pack. At daybreak on 16 June they marched south to Quatre Bras where a force under Marshal Ney was desperately being held by some Dutch-Belgians. Picton's men, among the first of the reinforcements, arrived at about two o'clock and were immediately brought into action, having to stand in line against French lancers because there was no time to form square. In this perilous position they still managed to repulse the lancers. Like Captain Fane and some other officers, there were men in the ranks who had met the French in Spain and Portugal, and their steadiness proved invaluable as fresh waves of cavalry assailed the shrinking squares of the 42nd and 44th. Later Wellington wrote in his dispatch: 'The troops of the fifth division and those of the Brunswick Corps were long and severely engaged, and conducted themselves with the utmost gallantry.' But for Mildmay the severe wound he received at Quatre Bras meant that he was not with the battalion at Waterloo two days later.

Henry and Mildmay both continued their military careers after the war was over. General Sir Henry Fane G.C.B. eventually became Commander-in-Chief in India. He died in 1840 on board the *Malabar*

Corunna Gold Medal (*left*) and Peninsular Gold Cross (*right*).

while on his way back to Europe and was buried at sea. Mildmay rose to lieutenant-general and lived on until 1860. He, like Charles, died unmarried but Henry left several children by the woman who was always known as Lady Fane, although, as his obituary quaintly phrases it, he married her 'privately'. On his death Fulbeck Hall passed to his eldest son, despite the circumstances of his parents' relationship. Eventually, the Hall would pass to the grandson of the Reverend Edward Fane, rector of Fulbeck, who must often have remembered his three soldier-brothers in his prayers as they did their duty in the best tradition of English gentlemen.

Researching the Fane Family

One of the advantages of researching men of the status of the Fanes is that their military service can be amplified by other details, often more personal and therefore more interesting than bald statements of fact, which have been passed down through the family. If the members of that family are willing to share this information, and no-one could have been more helpful than Mr Julian Fane, then the researcher's task becomes much easier. For example, a detailed family tree gave the dates and occupations of all eight brothers, including their time as Members of Parliament and the constituencies they represented. Henry was the only one of the soldier-brothers to enter Parliament, representing Lyme Regis from 1802–16, Sandwich from 1829–30 and Hastings from 1830–31. According to Mr Fane his politics were almost certainly of a Tory persuasion. The family tree also confirmed their close relationship to the Earls of Westmorland. The relationship of Lieutenant George Fane, killed at San Sebastian, to the family is more problematic. He does not appear on the family tree as a close relation, but the Ensign Fane to whom he left his effects has to be Mildmay because there was no other Ensign Fane in the army at that time. Family 'gossip' suggests that Sir Henry Fane, father of the three soldier brothers, had three illegitimate children, and it is certainly possible that George is connected in this way because the Fanes acknowledged and cared for their illegitimate offspring, one of Sir Henry's 'natural' sons even being brought up at Fulbeck Hall as a cousin.

Furthermore, chatting to someone like Mr Fane, who is fully conversant with his family history, can bring to light those details which

Fulbeck Hall.

otherwise lie concealed. The obituary to Henry Fane may refer to his 'private' marriage, but in fact there was no marriage as Isabella, daughter of an Irish gentleman, was already married.

To focus on military matters, a soldier as distinguished as Henry Fane appears in the memoirs of other participants of the war, humble soldiers like Harris and officers like Landmann, as well as in the more formal pages of the *Journal* of the Royal Dragoons. Also, the death of men like the Fanes was marked by an obituary, always a valuable source of information. For the Napoleonic period the *Gentleman's Magazine* is worth consulting, as in the case of Charles Fane, while an obituary to Henry Fane appeared in *The Times*. Such men can also be researched on internet sites like *Wikipedia* and *napoleon-series*. Finally, even if they died abroad, there will almost certainly be a memorial in their parish church. Compared to the men in the ranks, and even many officers, these men are visible to the researcher, often literally because there may well be a portrait, or portraits, of them. It is worth remembering, though, that portraits can pass out of the family and may be found in museums or private collections.

As for their military careers, the Army Lists trace all three brothers through their various transfers to different regiments and promotions, including onto the general list. The monthly returns (WO17) give a more detailed account of their circumstances, including Henry's period of leave spent attending Parliament and Charles' periods of sick leave which confirmed the serious nature of the wound he received at Corunna. For Henry's various commands in the Peninsula, though, an account of the wars, such as Oman's seven-volume work, gives the necessary detail to understand why he gained such an admirable reputation for competence.

Notes
1. *A Dorset Rifleman: The Recollections of Benjamin Harris*, p. 37.
2. Ibid., p. 58.
3. The *Gentleman's Magazine*, July 1813, p. 94.

Chapter Ten

WOMEN AT WAR
Biddy Skiddy and Agnes Reston

In 1810 the 94th Foot, stationed at Jersey, received orders for Portugal, a departure which necessitated one of the most distressing of army procedures. Joseph Donaldson wrote in his memoirs some years later:

> only six women to every hundred wives were allowed to accompany us. As there were, however, a great many more than that number, it was ordered that they should draw lots, to see who should remain. The women of the company to which I belonged were assembled in the pay-sergeant's room for that purpose. The men of the company gathered round them, to see the result, with various degrees of interest depicted on their countenances. The proportionate number of tickets were made with 'to go' or 'not to go' written on them. They were then placed in a hat, and the women were called by their seniority to draw their tickets. I looked round me before they began. It was an interesting scene. – The sergeant stood in the middle with a hat in his and, the women around him, with their hearts palpitating, and anxiety and suspence [sic] in every countenance. Here and there you would see the head of a married man pushed forward, from amongst the crowd, in the attitude of intense anxiety and attention.[1]

As an uninvolved spectator Donaldson could describe the scene dispassionately, but he still evinced sympathy for the women who drew 'not to go', the majority, so that the barracks were filled with the sound of unrestrained lamentation. There was more lamentation the following day:

> When we arrived where we were to embark, a most distressing scene took place, in the men parting from their wives. Some of

them indeed it did not appear to affect much: others had got themselves pretty nearly tipsy; but the most of them seemed to feel it acutely.[2]

Such scenes were enacted whenever a battalion was about to embark for service abroad, unless a regiment made a decision to take no women. Another spectator of the same procedure commented on the 'unusual decorum, and silence almost approaching melancholy'. In this instance it was the men

> who in turn quitted the ranks to advance to the centre; and I was surprised to hear the rattling of dice which were thrown on the drum-head, and the throws were frequently followed by a long drawing of breath as if it had been held for several minutes, and sometimes by a hysterical laugh of joyous certainty. Some had returned to their stations with a smile upon their faces; others sad and dejected; and every moment seemed to produce an increased excitement ... By some it was treated as a matter of indifference, but those were generally the successful parties; but to others it seemed the issue between life and death.[3]

This was particularly the case for the women hovering anxiously outside the circle of men.

For the women who drew 'not to go', or for whom the roll of the dice was contrary, the future was often bleak. Having been pro-vided by the regiment with money for the journey, they were then expected to return to the parish of their birth, where they would be supported by either their family or parish charity. Often neither source of welfare would be forthcoming. It is not surprising, there-fore, to find instances of women who remarried on the assumption that they had been widowed. Yet the experiences of women who accompanied their husbands to war may have been worse.

Even when the husband was on a home posting, the situation of his wife was unenviable. Very few senior officers welcomed the presence of women. Accommodation was likely to be a crowded barrack room, with only a blanket hung up to create some semblance of privacy. And if Donaldson is to be believed, there would be constant temp-tation towards immorality. However, once a wife accompanied her husband on active service, her difficulties multiplied as she under-went all the privations of life on campaign. If she had children, her problems could become even more desperate.

A woman might contribute to the communal life of the battalion by undertaking laundry and mending duties, for which she would probably receive a small amount of money; by cooking; and by tending the sick. At the same time she was not immune to the dangers of war. She could be taken prisoner, wounded or even killed. And death might lurk in the activities contemporaries associated with being a woman. Wheeler recorded the sad fate of a sergeant's wife who

> was nurse to the ward, she pricked her finger with a pin left in one of the bandages, caught the infection, her finger was first amputated, then her hand, the sluff appeared again in the stump, she refused to undergo another operation, the consequence was she soon died.[4]

Nothing, however, compared with the misery and suffering of a retreat. The memories of the men who trudged back to Corunna or struggled through the last few days of the retreat from Burgos inevitably contained images of suffering women and children. None were more harrowing than one recalled by Benjamin Harris:

> I remember another sight which I shall not forget to my dying day. Even now it causes me a sore heart to remember it. Soon after our halt beside the turnip-field, the screams of a child drew my attention to one of our women, who was endeavouring to drag along a little boy of about seven or eight years of age. The poor child was completely exhausted, his legs failing under him. Up to this moment, the mother had occasionally been assisted by some of the men, who had taken it in turns to help the little fellow on, but now all appeal was in vain. No man had more strength than that necessary for the support of his own carcass. Although the mother could no longer raise the child in her arms – as her reeling pace too plainly showed – still she continued to drag the child along with her. It was a pitiable sight, and it was wonderful to behold the efforts the poor woman made to keep the boy amongst us, even though she was like a moving corpse herself. At last, the little fellow had no strength even to cry. With mouth wide open, he stumbled onwards until they both sank down to rise no more. When the shades of evening came down, they were far behind, amongst the dead and dying.[5]

When the army was in retreat women were an impediment; but there were other ways in which they could plague commanding officers:

> A multitude of soldiers' wives stuck to the army like bricks. Averse to all military discipline, they impeded our progress at times very much ... They were under no control, and were first mounted up and away in advance, blocking up narrow passages, and checking the advance of the army with their donkeys, after repeated orders to follow in the rear of their respective corps, or their donkeys would be shot.[6]

They were also voracious plunderers, or foragers, to use a kinder word, who provoked Wellington to issue a series of general orders aimed to control their misbehaviour. For example, at Medellin on 23 October 1809 he instructed that

> Officers commanding divisions and brigades will be pleased to take measures to prevent the women, and followers of the army, from buying up the bread which is prepared for the soldiers' rations. This practice, carried on in the irregular manner it is at present, must ultimately prejudice the soldiers, and prevent the regular supply of bread.

Women with the baggage. (*National Army Museum*)

Three years later the same problem led him to order that 'The followers of the army ... must be prevented by the provosts from plundering the gardens and fields of vegetables. The women must be informed that they must obey orders, or they will be turned out of the army.'

One such termagant, immune to the power of commanding officers, the provost, or Wellington himself, was Mrs Biddy Skiddy, who lives on in the memoirs of George Bell of the 34th Foot. She first appears as one of those who stuck to the army like bricks. Invited by another wife to ignore the latest command to keep to the rear of the column, she

> led the way on her celebrated donkey called the 'Queen of Spain'. She was a squat little Irishwoman, and broad as a big turtle. 'Dhrive on, girls, and we'll bate them to the end ov this day, at any rate,' says Mother Skiddy.

On this occasion circumstances were against the women. The Provost-Marshal was waiting for them, and ordered shots to be fired at the donkeys,

> killing and wounding two or three *pour exemple*. There was a wild, fierce, and furious yell struck up at once, with more weeping and lamentation than one generally hears at an Irish funeral, with sundry prayers for the vagabond that murdered the lives of these poor, darling, innocent crathers![7]

Those who had lost their beasts of burden gathered as much of their baggage as they could carry or loaded it on the Queen of Spain at Mrs Skiddy's invitation, and trudged along with the troops, still cursing the Provost-Marshal. Yet the next morning, nothing deterred, Mrs Skiddy and her fellows were once more at the front of the march.

The problem for the authorities was that they failed to appreciate the strength of feeling that motivated women like Biddy Skiddy. Forget loyalty to the army. It was their husbands' comfort that over-rode all other considerations:

> 'We must risk something to be in before the men, to have the fire an' a dhrop of tay ready for the poor crathers after their load an' their labour. An' sure if I went in the rare, the French, bad luck to them, wud pick me up, me an' me donkey, and then Dan would be lost entirely?' She was a devoted soldier's wife, and a right

good one, an excellent forager, and never failed to have something for Dan when we were all starving.

Indeed, Daniel Skiddy, no bigger than his wife, 'short and stumpy, but with great bone and pluck, and of good character'[8], was lucky to have such a woman by his side.

This was demonstrated during the retreat to Portugal in 1812 when, as she told Bell,

Yer honour minds how we were all kilt an' destroyed on the long march last winter and the French at our heels, an' all our men droppin' and dyin' on the roadside, waitin' to be killed all over agin by them vagabonds comin' after us. Well, I don't know if you seed him, sir, but down drops poor Dan, to be murdered like all the rest. Says he, 'Biddy dear, I can't go on furder one yard to save me life!'

'O, Dan jewel,' sis I, 'I'll help you on a bit; tak' a hould av me, an' throw away your knapsack.'

'I'll niver part wid' me knapsack,' says he, 'nor my firelock, while I'm a soger.'

'Dogs then,' sis I, 'you 'ont live long, for the French are comin' up quick upon us.' Thinkin', you see, sir, to give him sperret to move, but the poor crather hadn't power to stir a lim'. Now, I heard the firing behind an' saw them killin' Dan, as if it was! So I draws him up on the bank, for, sis I, 'the French will have ye in half an hour, an' me too, the pagans!' In truth I was just thinkin' they had hould av us both, when I draws him up on me back, knapsack an' all. 'Throw away your gun,' sis I.

'I won't,' says he. 'Biddy, I'll shoot the first vagabond lays hould av your tail,' says he. He always was a conthrary crather when any one invaded his firelock.

Well, sir, I went away wid him on me back, knapsack, firelock, an' all, as strong as Sampson, for the fear I was in. An' fegs, I carried him half a league after the regiment into the bivwack. Me back was bruck entirely from that time to this, an' it'll never get strait till I go to the Holy Well in Ireland, an' have Father McShane's blessin', an' his hand laid over me! An' that's all the thruth, yer honour, I've told ye.[9]

This devotion to her husband, worthy fellow that he was, inevitably provoked some teasing. On one occasion, after the action at St Pierre,

Biddy Skiddy. *(National Army Museum)*

when she was desperately searching for Dan, she was told that 'he's run away wid a French lady he tuck in the battle'. She brushed this aside with the riposte, 'An' he'll spake Irish to her,' before returning to her principal concern, to find Dan. Told that he had suffered a broken leg, she went off to comfort him, 'bellowing to the shambles'.[10]

On finally parting from Biddy Skiddy at the end of the war in the Peninsula, Bell told her that she was a wonderful woman whose good behaviour was recognised by the whole regiment. Then 'I bid this wonderful structure of humanity a friendly farewell, after squaring with her for a year's washing and darning.'[11] She was reluctant to take the money. After her loyalty to her husband, nothing was as strong as her loyalty to the regiment. Bell belonged to her company and was welcome to a bit of washing.

If Biddy Skiddy demonstrated devotion to her husband, Agnes Reston displayed devotion to duty worthy of any soldier. A young officer was

> struck by the coolness of women [before a battle]. You seldom hear a single expression of alarm escape them; indeed, they become, probably from habit, and from the example of others, to the full as indifferent to danger as their husbands.[12]

But the indifference to danger displayed by Mrs Reston was nothing less than heroic.

Agnes, née Harkness, was Scottish, born in 1771. She married James Reston, who rose to sergeant in the 94th Foot. She was one of the women who drew 'to go' in the wives lottery in Jersey, and sailed with her husband and 4-year-old son first to Lisbon and then on to Cadiz. In February 1810, when the 94th arrived, Cadiz was newly under siege and Marshal Victor was seeking to establish batteries along the shore line. If he took possession of Fort Matagorda, he would be able to bombard and possibly take Fort Puntales, from which Cadiz itself would be vulnerable to his guns. To prevent this, a body of men from the 94th, accompanied by a detachment of artillery and some sailors and marines, in total about 150 men, were ferried across to establish an allied battery at Matagorda.

They found themselves in a fort that had been all but destroyed by British naval guns when the French first advanced on Cadiz. Consequently, once their guns had been mounted and had destroyed the nearest French battery, the detachment set to work building parapets and laying more gun platforms. Eventually, six guns and two mortars were hauled into place, while further support was afforded by a Spanish man-of-war and six or more gunboats. With this fire-power they were able to hold the French at bay for nearly two months.

Marshal Victor, however, was only too aware of the strategic importance of Matagorda and eventually launched a concentrated attack. His gunners soon had their range, causing steadily increasing losses among the small defending force. The dead were left where they fell, but the wounded were carried to the shelter of the bomb-proof. Donaldson takes up the story:

> The firing on both sides had been kept up without intermission from two o'clock in the morning; but as it now became dark, it was partially suspended. I then, for the first time, ventured to go below to the bomb-proof. The scene there was dismal – the wounded filled the whole place, and the doctor had not got through with the dressing of them. In this he was materially assisted from the commencement of the action by a female (Mrs Reston) who had removed her little son to the safety of the bomb-proof before offering her help to the surgeon, Mr Bennet. There was a shortage of bandages, so she tore up her own and her husband's linen for the purpose.[13]

Sergeant Reston had been chosen for the Matagorda detachment, and his wife and child accompanied him, although no-one would have criticised her if she had opted to remain safely in Cadiz. Nor was tending the wounded the full extent of the services she rendered to the beleaguered garrison. As the French bombardment intensified and the number of wounded increased, the supply of water in the bomb-proof ran low. The surgeon ordered a drummer-boy to leave the safety of the shelter and draw some more water from the well. Not surprisingly, the lad was transfixed by fear and remained immobile even when the surgeon gave him the order for a second time.

Mrs Reston did not hesitate. 'The poor thing's frightened, and no wonder at it ... Give it to me and I'll go.' Despite the French bombardment, she successfully filled the bucket but before she could draw it out of the well a stray shot severed the rope. With the aid of a sailor she was able to recover the bucket and bring it to the surface, all the while under fire. She brought the water back to the bomb-proof and continued to help the surgeon. In addition, she carried sandbags to shore up the defences, brought ammunition to the guns, and wine and water to the exhausted gunners. Even when Matagorda became untenable she made three crossings to Cadiz, not only to get her child to safety but also to save all she could of her family's possessions. Donaldson retained an image of Agnes Reston, 'while the shot and shells were flying thick around her, bending her body over [her child] to shield it from the danger by the exposure of her own person'.[14]

Such exceptional courage and devotion should have earned some reward, but the later treatment of Agnes Reston only serves to demonstrate how little women were valued by the army. As Donaldson commented:

> It is a matter of surprise to many, that the courage she displayed and the services she rendered on that occasion, should have been entirely overlooked by those who had the power of rewarding her; or that her claims on the country were not more warmly seconded by the officer who commanded in the fort.[15]

James Reston eventually retired on a sergeant's pension of 1/10d a day, on which he and his wife struggled to survive. There was no son to support them. After enlisting into the 94th, the lad became a victim of bullying. He retaliated, was flogged for insubordination, deserted and disappeared from his parents' lives. When James Reston became too infirm to work, Agnes applied for assistance. She had the support of the regimental officers and the recommendation of the Commander-in-Chief, but the Secretary for War maintained there were no funds available for a merely charitable purpose.

Her husband died in 1834 and the pension died with him, so that Agnes became a pauper. By 1844 she was resident in the Town's Hospital, Glasgow, where she earned a pittance as a nurse, even though she was now 72. A year later Donaldson published a revised edition of his memoirs, bringing her unrewarded heroism to public attention. A committee of officers now launched a public appeal to which even Queen Victoria donated, and enough money was raised to guarantee Agnes an annuity of £30 a year. This gave her financial security, although she chose to remain in the hospital and gave any surplus money to charity.

Agnes Reston died on Christmas Eve 1856 and was buried with her husband in Glasgow's Southern Necropolis. The inscription on their gravestone reads: 'In memory of James Reston, late serjeant 94th Regiment, who died on the 24th day of October, 1834, aged 63 years, and of Agnes Harkness, his wife, "The Heroine of Matagorda", who died 24 December 1856, aged 85 years.'

Researching women at war

Researching the women who accompanied their husbands to war is particularly challenging. Although journals and memoirs are full of references to their presence, often highly critical, the official records tend to preserve their anonymity. It was 1863 before the musters listed by name the women for whom accommodation was provided, and 1883 before the simple fact that a man was married was included on his discharge papers. Earlier musters enumerate the number of women and children with the battalion, because money was required to feed them, but they are not named individually.

It is possible, if a man survived long enough, that by searching the 1841 and 1851 census returns (available online) the researcher will be able to establish that he was married while he was in the army, the ages of his children offering some supporting evidence. This is conditional on a range of circumstances, however, and even then will not reveal whether the wife accompanied him abroad.

Women sometimes appear by name in the records. The muster of the 30th Foot for January 1809 contains a list of women on an inserted form detailing the money that was paid to them to return home. This is negative evidence, however, because these were the women who drew 'not to go'. With the KGL musters for 1809 are some loose sheets of paper which name the women who were drawing half-rations (and quarter-rations for their children) during the Corunna campaign. These women appear again as drawing more money when (unlike the majority) they obeyed Sir John Moore and returned to Lisbon, and then to England, before the retreat commenced. In each case there is a reference to the woman's age and a brief physical description.

A further indication that a women was with her husband may be found in casualty returns (WO25), or sometimes in the musters, when the details of a man's will reveal that he left his money to his wife 'at the regiment'. The unfortunate Mrs Mary Murphy, whose husband was a colour sergeant in the 30th, received money 'at the regiment' three times, from her husband and both her sons. She also appears on another, much earlier list, of wives who accompanied their husbands to sea while they were serving as marines in the 1790s.

Nevertheless, such means of establishing whether a man was married, and whether his wife accompanied him on active service, are at best random and fortuitous. As a result, the rare case of a memoirist who includes information about named battalion wives (as Harris, Bell and Donaldson do) is particularly to be valued.

The two women who have been considered here were obviously out of the ordinary. Mrs Skiddy, with her devotion to her husband and disregard for authority lives on in the pages of George Bell's memoirs, fashioned from the diary he kept. The young ensign was only 18 when he first encountered her, a callow youth, which probably explains why he was so overawed by this generous-hearted termagant whom he named 'Mrs Commissary-General Skiddy' as a compliment to her foraging skills.

Joseph Donaldson was sympathetic to the plight of army wives. Time and again he wrote compassionately about their tribulations, as in his extended account of the drawing of lots (only part of which has been quoted here) or his description of their sufferings during the retreat from Burgos. Without this sympathetic interest it is unlikely that the heroism of Agnes Reston would have been known beyond the regiment. Her actions made her a heroine: Donaldson's memoirs made her a public heroine of the kind so beloved of the Victorians. This in turn brought her comfort in her old age. It also means she can be accessed on the internet, where there are not only accounts of her life, but an article from the *Glasgow Herald* detailing subscriptions already received and some (excruciatingly bad) verses by William McGonagall entitled *The Heroine of Matagorda*.

Notes

1. Donaldson, *The Eventful Life of a Soldier*, pp. 80–1.
2. Ibid., p. 86.
3. Flexible Grommet, 'Leaves from Log-Book', *United Services Journal*, 1834, pp. 487–8.
4. *The Letters of Private Wheeler*, p. 15.
5. *A Dorset Rifleman: The Recollections of Benjamin Harris*, pp. 110–11.
6. Bell, *Soldier's Glory*, p. 60.
7. Ibid., p. 60.
8. Ibid., pp. 60–1.
9. Ibid., pp. 146–7.
10. Ibid., p. 115.
11. Ibid., p. 147.
12. Gleig, *The Subaltern*, p. 123.
13. Donaldson, p. 117.
14. Donaldson, *The Recollections of a Soldier*, p. 359.
15. Donaldson, *The Eventful Life of a Soldier*, p. 118.

Chapter Eleven

THE 'KING'S HARD BARGAINS'

Samuel Lickler and Richard Key of the 30th Foot

E very regiment had them, a hard core of incorrigibles who were resistant to army discipline and could not be tamed by the often ferocious military discipline of the period. John Colborne, lieutenant-colonel of the 52nd, one of the most distinguished of the Peninsular regiments, was a captain in the 20th Foot during the retreat to Corunna. Years later, he was reflecting on the retreat, and particularly on the problem of straggling, which he identified as an incurable disease. 'The system of recruiting is so defective and so radically bad in every regiment we must say there are from 50 to 100 bad characters that neither punishment nor any kind of discipline can restrain.'[1] Such men took every opportunity to stray from the ranks, often in pursuit of drink or plunder.

Even soldiers like Benjamin Harris, who strongly disliked the brutality of corporal punishment, acknowledged that it was the only effective means of controlling the 'king's hard bargains'. These were the men who made work for the provosts and whose names litter the pages of courts-martial records. And like bad apples, they could corrupt those around them.

It would be simplistic to assume, however, that the men who proved the worst delinquents were the 'scum of the earth' (to use Wellington's famous phrase) when they joined the army. Undoubtedly a fair number came from the dregs of society, while some of the crimes committed, like quite sophisticated house-breaking, suggested their background was a criminal milieu. There are cases, though, of men who were depraved by the conditions of service they subsequently encountered. Two such men were Samuel Lickler and Richard Key of the 30th Foot.

After the collapse of the Peace of Amiens in 1803 the British government found itself facing a severe manpower shortage in the army. (Too many second battalions and high number regiments had been disbanded at the first hint of peace.) One solution was to establish the Army of Reserve, a balloted force which was then allocated among the regular regiments of the line, the means by which Benjamin Harris was sent to the 66th. Another solution was to permit the enlistment of a certain number of boys per battalion. The 30th received the first of a steady intake of boys in February 1805. Five months later, Samuel Lickler arrived in the second battalion of the regiment as part of a forty-five-strong detachment from the Army of Defence, the successor force to the Army of Reserve. His age is not given in the records, but within a few months he was returned as 'from boy', meaning that he had reached 16, the point at which he became a lad.

Men from the Army of Defence were often of doubtful quality, although this was generally in terms of age and fitness. There is certainly nothing to suggest that young Samuel was anything less than a promising and willing addition to the ranks, particularly as he quickly enlisted for general service. He was also selected for transfer to the first battalion, in theory the repository of the better men, in April 1806. Within a few weeks of joining them he was on his way to India.

There is no sure way of identifying when he first transgressed because records of regimental courts martial were not recorded in official documents until 1812. His first recorded appearance occurred early in that year when he received 200 lashes for unsoldierlike conduct, an indefinite charge which could cover a multitude of offences. India provided particular temptations, however, to idle soldiers, the worst of which were drink (arrack) and women. In an alien culture and unpleasant conditions they represented the best means of escape from the tedium of garrison life. Lickler definitely seems to have succumbed to the first of these temptations once his conduct went to the bad.[2]

His next recorded offence sometime in the six-month period between November 1812 and May 1813 was being absent from quarters and making away with his regimental necessaries. In India these were: a watch coat and forage cap, three shirts, a black leather stock, three pairs of socks or stockings, two pairs of cloth gaiters, three pairs of shoes, shoe brushes and other equipment for keeping the uniform smart, and worm, brush, picker and turn screw for the musket. Necessaries were inspected every Monday, and a man who lost, damaged or, more likely, sold them was tried by regimental court martial and punished. Lickler's sentence was 200 lashes and stoppages, money taken from his pay until he made good the value of the missing necessaries. Had he been in the second battalion and committed these offences (although they were rare in that battalion) he would probably have been spared some of the lashes, or even have been given a lighter sentence for what appears to have been a first offence. This was India, though, where misbehaviour was an ongoing problem, so there was no leniency.

Regimental courts-martial records are not dated, so it is impossible to know how quickly Lickler re-offended, although it was in the same six-month period. This time the charge was making away with part of his necessaries, which would suggest that on the previous occasion he had disposed of them all. He received the same sentence, as he did on the next occasion he faced a court martial, for repeated drunkenness. In other words, he had received 600 lashes in six months. The third offence, coupled with the supposition that he had sold his necessaries, suggests that the common thread was drink. Yet a flogging was a gruesome experience, both for those who suffered it

The lash. (*Author's collection*)

A Victorian image of a military flogging. (*Philip Haythornthwaite*)

and those who had to watch, and it seems almost incredible that any man could keep on offending when he knew what fate awaited him, unless the lure of alcohol was so strong that it deprived him of any sense of crime followed by inevitable punishment.

Such might be a valid conclusion in Lickler's case, except that having apparently become a typical 'hard bargain', Lickler was able to keep himself out of trouble for two years. Then, in the register for May to October 1816 his name was back on the list of offenders, this time for once again being absent without leave and making away with his regimental necessaries. The punishment was now 300 lashes and stoppages.

In December Lickler faced a regimental general court martial, that is to say a trial before a court with the sentencing powers of a general court martial, which included up to 1,200 lashes and death, but comprising officers of his own regiment. This could prove distinctly disadvantageous, since these men would know him all too well. The charge was that he had quitted the fort (St George, Madras) when on guard and had not returned until the following day, and only then because he was brought back as a prisoner. In other words, it was assumed that he had made an attempt to desert. He was also charged with making away with the chief part of his necessaries.

Invited to plead, Lickler immediately pleaded guilty, which meant there was no need to call any witnesses and sentence could be pronounced:

> The court finds the prisoner Samuel Lickler guilty by his own confession, and by virtue of the Articles of War do therefore sentence him to receive a punishment of five hundred lashes, at such time and place and in such manner as the approving officer may please to direct. To be put under stoppages not exceeding the half of his pay until he makes good the necessaries deficient.

On this occasion, however, the approving officer, a senior officer who confirmed or questioned the sentence, was not pleased to direct. Colonel Ogg, commanding the troops in the garrison of Fort St George was concerned that there had been no examination of evidence. As he pointed out, actually echoing the instruction of the Judge Advocate in London, 'A man through ignorance may plead guilty to a charge which when examined into may be found accompanied by circumstances that in some degree extenuate the guilt. I will thank you to let evidence be taken in this trial.' This is a reminder that, however brutal the nature of military punishment, the administration of military justice was scrupulously disinterested.[3]

Nevertheless, the court responded by pointing out that the prisoner had persisted in pleading guilty, which implies that the court had tried to persuade him to enter a plea of not guilty so that evidence could be heard. To support their decision, they referred to the work of Alexander Fraser Tytler, whose book, *An Essay on Military Law and the Practice of Courts Martial*, seems to have been used as a handbook. Tytler advocated that when a man could not be persuaded against a guilty plea the court was not required to hear evidence. Colonel Ogg accepted this but he halved the sentence.

By this point it would seem that Lickler was intent only on escaping from the army. Two desertions within a matter of days, the second before he could be tried for the first offence, led to another regimental court martial. This time the court took their best means of getting rid of an unsatisfactory soldier, short of executing him, and ordered that Lickler should be transported for life.

The notable point about Lickler's many offences is that the only sufferer was the man himself. This is very different from Richard Key, one of the hardest cases in the 30th. Yet, like Lickler, there was nothing at first to suggest that Key would become such a problem to the regiment. He came from the small village of Westborough in Lincolnshire, and enlisted at Sleaford on 26 January. By April he was with the first battalion, set for service in India. This must initially have seemed to promise the action which most soldiers hoped for, when he spent four weeks on Prince of Wales Island as part of a detachment for marine service. The call to service never came, though, and the detachment then continued on to India, where Key was appointed drummer, with an extra 1d a day and some status in the battalion. In this position he would have been involved in the flogging of offenders, and that may have kept him from temptation because it was not until January 1811 that he was recorded as a prisoner in the guard room. His offence must have been trivial or unproven because he remained a drummer. In August 1812, however, he was demoted to the ranks for rioting in the barracks and making away with part of his necessaries. His punishment, like Lickler's for similar offences, was 200 lashes and stoppages.

After this, his descent into regular offender was fairly rapid, but it is the nature of his crimes and the means the battalion used to punish him which are interesting. His next recorded offence, committed sometime in the first half of 1813, involved the maltreatment of a sepoy, for which he was sentenced to two weeks in solitary confinement. In the same period there was a charge of unsoldierlike conduct, punished by 100 lashes and two months' extra drill. The drill suggests shortcomings in the way he was performing as a soldier. In the second half of the year there was a more serious charge, striking a corporal, which earned him another two weeks in solitary confinement. By the end of 1814, a clear picture emerges of an unmanageable individual given to acts of violence.

The register produced in June 1815 confirms this impression. He was court-martialled twice, the second time for unsoldierlike conduct and maltreating a native woman, for which he was sentenced to 100 lashes. Before that he had been found guilty of avoiding a march on the pretence of a lame ankle; another 100 lashes. The next year he managed two more regimental courts martial, for quitting the fort when in the surgeon's report (200 lashes) and, once again, for striking a corporal (300 lashes). The first of these offences is interesting

A court martial. (*Author's collection*)

because if he was in the surgeon's report then he was unfit for duty. Combined with the lame ankle the previous year it suggests Key malingered as a means of avoiding duty. The second, of course, demonstrates his tendency to use violence.

At the end of 1816 he faced a general regimental court martial for what is probably the most bizarre of all his offences. Having left the fort without leave, he got drunk and rioted in Blacktown, an area of Madras. He then divested himself of his clothes. When a sergeant intervened to arrest him he reacted in a way that seems to have been instinctive by this point. He struck the sergeant a violent blow to the head. Not surprisingly, he was sentenced to 600 lashes.

So it went on. In June 1817 he appeared in the regimental court facing three charges: resisting arrest, leaving the hospital where he was a patient and not returning until the following day, when he was brought back drunk, and then wilfully destroying his bed and the windows of the guard room. The sentence was three weeks of solitary confinement and stoppages, which obviously had no effect because a month later he was back in court. This time it was merely leaving the fort without permission and not returning until brought back as a prisoner two days later. There followed six weeks in solitary confinement. Immediately upon release, however, he refused to go on guard duty when ordered by the orderly sergeant and also refused to get ready for muster, for which he received 200 lashes. In October he was back before a general regimental court martial, charged with mutiny, which put him in solitary confinement for another three months. One has to conclude that the advantage of confining him was that it at least kept him out of the courts, and out of the way of those who had to deal with him on a daily basis.

Strangely enough, although Key did not undergo a conversion to good behaviour, his offences became less frequent at this point. There were no appearances in 1818. In October 1819 he was charged with breaking his log (a means of restraining soldiers) and leaving the fort, and then when he came back, telling the corporal on duty he was damned if he would be logged. No sentence is recorded, which suggests that the court dismissed the charges. His next appearance was in July 1820 when his unsoldierlike conduct was defined as leaving the fort at night and ill-treating a native woman. He was additionally charged with running away from the sergeant who had been sent to arrest him. The punishment was a month in solitary confinement. Then in March 1821 he made his last appearance. This time the charges were refusing to attend evening parade, striking the corporal who ordered him to the guard room and showing insolence and disrespect to an officer on regimental parade. He was sentenced to 300 lashes, but this was commuted to six weeks' solitary confinement.

One can only conclude that there must have been great relief in the regiment when Richard Key died on 18 June 1822 in the regimental hospital. He was actually owed over £6, but since there was no known next-of-kin the money remained with the army, rather less probably than he owed them in terms of the trouble he had caused.

It is difficult to offer much defence for either Lickler or Key, yet the thought remains, would either of them have become 'hard bargains' if they had served with the second battalion in the Peninsula and Flanders, instead of being sent to India with its dangerous combination of tedium and temptation?

Researching Samuel Lickler and Richard Key

Like the other men and NCOs in these case studies, the careers of Samuel Lickler and Richard Key can be reconstructed from the muster rolls. These records, however, do not reveal that either man was a 'hard bargain', although the coincidence of Richard Key being returned as a prisoner on 25 January 1811, the day of the muster, is the first suggestion of misbehaviour on his part. In order to establish both the frequency and the nature of the two men's offences it is necessary to consult the bi-annual inspection returns, which can be found in WO27. Their arrangement is rather random within the parameters of each year, and some returns have been lost, but where they exist they create a pen-picture of a battalion, including after 1811 details of regimental courts martial. These identify the name of the offender, the charge or charges against him, the sentence of the court and the punishment actually inflicted.

The records within the inspection returns also indicate where a man has been tried by general (including general regimental) court martial. If this is the case, then there is a good chance that the proceedings can be found in WO71. Again the arrangement is by year. Opening a box of court-martial papers for the first time can be a somewhat off-putting moment, but it is worth looking carefully at the folded-up and somewhat grimy contents since the verbatim proceedings themselves give a word by word account of what happened.

Men like Lickler and Key, who cannot be found in WO97, are difficult to trace beyond their military experiences. For Lickler's life after 1817 it becomes necessary to explore transportation records. HO11 records the individual convict ships and the names of the convicts, plus date and place of conviction, but does not necessarily cover soldiers from India. HO10 contains census returns for Australia, where Lickler was sent. The 1828 census includes how the individual came to Australia. Consulting ancestry.aus revealed that he went from Madras to Australia on the naval vessel HMS *Guide* in 1818 as a 'ticket of leave' man, that is, released but under some restrictions. A search of death records revealed only one Samuel Lickler, registered at Gundaroo Gunning, Yass, New South Wales in 1884. His age was given as 62, a few years older than his military records suggest, but age was often a matter of guesswork, particularly for a man who was on the other side of the world from his parish records in Cheshire.

Key is a similar problem, but some conclusions can be drawn about him by adopting a more lateral approach. WO97 records for the 30th Foot include a William Key who, like Richard, came from Westborough, little more than a hamlet, in Lincolnshire, and attested on the same date as Richard. This suggests that they were brothers, or possibly cousins. Unfortunately, William was discharged in 1821, a year before Richard died. Had he still been in India, we could have been sure that he was Richard's next-of-kin because the relationship would have been stated in the casualty lists.

William Key was 15 when he enlisted. Richard could have been older or younger, but the fact that he was appointed drummer would suggest that in 1807 he was still either a boy (not yet 16) or a lad (not yet 18). William's occupation was given as labourer, as was Richard's in the casualty returns (WO25), indicating their agricultural background. An interesting point about William was his height. At 6 feet 3 inches tall, he was a good 8 inches above the average. If Richard was of a similar height it may explain why he found violence such an instinctive response. To use a phrase, he was merely throwing his weight around.

William Key was not without blemish. His discharge papers describe him as 'generally well conducted' but he was twice brought before a regimental court martial. In the June 1815 register he appears as charged with unsoldierlike conduct, mistreating a bazaar man. He was sentenced to fifty lashes, but pardoned for good conduct. A year later he struck a corporal and received 300 lashes. There is a suggestion here that like Richard he was inclined to react violently, but his two offences pale into insignificance beside what can only be described as the vicious delinquency of Richard Key.

Notes

1. John Colborne, *A Singular Talent for War*, p. 250.
2. The effect of India on the conduct of the soldiers serving there is demonstrated by a comparison with 2/30th, who remained in Europe and saw service in the Peninsula and Flanders. The frequency of regimental courts martial in the second battalion was less than a quarter that of the first battalion.
3. Lieutenant-Colonel Richard Archdall, 40th Foot, was court-martialled at Lamego in 1813 and dismissed the service for unauthorised use of the lash.

FURTHER READING

Most of the material in these case studies was obtained from primary sources. That which came from official documents has been identified in the 'Researching' sections. Below are listed the other primary sources. An asterisk indicates those that are still in print or easily obtainable second-hand.

George Bell, *Soldier's Glory* (reprinted 1991) – a version of Bell's Peninsular experience is available as *Ensign Bell in the Peninsula*.
Edward Costello (ed. Eileen Hathaway), *The True Story of a Peninsular Rifleman* (1997) – other editions of Costello's memoirs are available.
*Joseph Donaldson, *The Eventful Life of a Soldier* (1827).
Benjamin Harris (ed. Eileen Hathaway), *A Dorset Rifleman* (1996) – Harris's memoirs can be obtained in several different editions.
*Friedrich Lindau (eds James Bogle and Andrew Uffindell), *A Waterloo Hero* (2009).
Benjamin Miller, *The Adventures of Serjeant Benjamin Miller* (A Naval and Military Press publication, undated).
*Daniel Nicol, *Sergeant Nicol: the experiences of a Gordon Highlander during the Napoleonic Wars in Egypt, the Peninsula and France*.
William Verner (ed. Ruth Verner), *Reminiscences of William Verner 1782–1871* (1965).
*William Wheeler (ed. B.H. Liddell Hart), *The Letters of Private Wheeler 1809–1828*.

The experiences of Major George Baring and other officers of the KGL light battalions at Waterloo can be found in Gareth Glover, *The Waterloo Archive*, Volume II (2010) and John Franklin, *Waterloo Hanoverian Correspondence* (2010).

The letters of Robert Cairnes were originally printed in 1905 in *The Dickson Manuscripts*, edited by Major J.H. Leslie, and were reprinted by Ken Trotman in 1991.

The journals of Edward Hodge (7th Hussars), Andrew Hartley (Royal Horse Guards) and Edward Neville Macready (30th Foot) are at present unpublished.

The number of books that have been written on the Revolutionary and Napoleonic Wars over the last two centuries is large enough to fill several sizeable volumes of bibliography but certain of them will prove useful to anyone wanting to find out more about an ancestor's experiences during these wars. Volumes IV–XI of the Hon. J.W. Fortescue's monumental *History of the British Army*, available as a Naval and Military Press reprint, cover the whole period. The two classic texts which focus on the Peninsular War are William Napier's six-volume *History of the War in the Peninsula and the South of France* and Sir Charles Oman's seven-volume *History of the Peninsular War*. Although they are not likely to be read in their entirety, except by the enthusiast with stamina, all three sets are worth dipping into.

A modern one-volume study of the period is *The War of Wars* by Charles Harvey, while Charles Esdaile has written *The Peninsular War, a New History*. Specific treatments of the battle of Waterloo have been produced by Mark Adkin (*A Waterloo Companion* – which tells you all you could want to know about the battle), Andrew Roberts (*Waterloo* – a succinct account), David Howarth (*Waterloo: A Near Run Thing*), and Ian Fletcher (*A Desperate Business*). These suggestions, however, merely touch the surface of what is available.

There are books that take a wider perspective such as *The Armies of Wellington* by Philip Haythornthwaite, *Life in Wellington's Army* by Antony Brett-James, and Peter Snow's recently-published *To War with Wellington*. More specialised, but equally valuable, are Ian Fletcher's *Galloping at Everything*, a reappraisal of the cavalry, *Following the Drum* by Brigadier E.C.G. Page, which considers the experiences of the women who accompanied the army, and *Rifles*, by Mark Urban. Again, these are just starting-points. Go into any bookshop, new, second-hand or antiquarian and you will undoubtedly discover many other books that will take you into the world of your military forebears.

INDEX